THE HIGH-TICKET METHOD®

THE HIGH-TICKET METHOD®

THE POWER OF PREMIUM:
HIGH-TICKET STRATEGIES THAT MULTIPLY
YOUR BUSINESS AND INCOME... ETHICALLY

DR TANIA KING-MOHAMMAD

authors
AND CO.

To Luna, Giovanna, my mum, Estelle, my dad, Saif and my husband Rapha. I love you all so deeply. Thank you for always believing in me, I couldn't have done this without you.

CONTENTS

FOREWORD

I've worked with thousands of coaches, strategists, advisors and the like over the last decade, both as clients and mentors. Throughout this time, I've noticed that some phrases pop up regularly. Lots are fluffy and lots are done to death, some are more useful than others, but one that I hear consistently is High-Ticket – as in 'Your High-Ticket Offer' or 'High-Ticket Sales'.

But what does this actually mean?

Well, if I'm honest, it lost much of its meaning due to misuse in the industry. Get-rich-quick schemes, MLMs, ridiculously inflated prices and outdated and sleazy sales methods are everywhere online and have tarnished the phrase. But the good news is that Tania gets it and Tania nails it.

As she rightly says, *"High-ticket sales does not mean adding another zero to the end of your price point,"* and her understanding of this is what sets her apart from so many others.

Since I met Tania, I have seen her grow. I have seen her epiphanies along the way as she realised that she needed to reassess her business model to one that saw her hit her first £100K sales month in under three years.

I have seen her implement systems and strategies that work and set her apart.

But aside from her knowledge, her experience, her personality, her intelligence and her relatability, what really sets her apart are two small but oh-so-important words:

Authenticity and ethics.

She knows exactly what works and what doesn't when it comes to high-ticket client attraction and sales and has managed to impart her knowledge in this book, which is crammed with implementable nuggets to steer you on your path to high-ticket success.

What's more, she has done it in a way that means no sleaze, no smarmy tactics involved and absolutely nothing that will leave you with an icky taste in your mouth. I love her for this.

I also love that she is not afraid to talk about money! If you've been playing too small for too long and want to get seen, hired and paid as the go-to expert for high-paying, premium clients then you need to read this book. I'm excited for you to read it and for many more to work with Tania to change their own lives and gain financial freedom.

Believe me, you're learning from the best.

Lisa Johnson

INTRODUCTION: GETTING STARTED

What if I told you that everything you've been taught about success—working harder, hustling longer, sacrificing more—is wrong? And what if I told you that you could make what most would call 'illogical amounts of money'—but in a way that feels authentic, aligned, and deeply fulfilling?

You see others consistently converting the fast-moving, high-paying clients you truly want to work with, being paid much higher rates than you're currently charging, and you'd love to be one of those people.

Your business is doing great, but you feel stuck, unsure how to take things to the next level. You're not sure what makes an irresistible high-ticket offer and if you're really honest with yourself, you know you're still not speaking to the high-caliber, high-ticket clients you want to attract and work with.

If you're an established entrepreneur who wants to get paid more for the work you love by creating and selling the right high-ticket offers to attract premium clients, while genuinely and ethically transforming their lives or businesses, this book is for you. And I'm ecstatic for you to dive in because I know the huge impact this will have.

It's time for you to be seen, hired and paid as the go-to expert for high-ticket clients in your industry. This book is the vehicle to help you do exactly that. It's here to help you get paid more for the work you love without increasing your workload, by mastering high-ticket client attraction and sales, ethically.

In this book, I'll share the exact methodology that underpins all the work I do with clients who are ready to attract higher-paying, faster-moving clients into their businesses to multiply their impact and income, and ultimately to live the freedom-based lifestyle they want. It will take you step-by-step through *The High-Ticket Method*®. This is my six-step system that helped me achieve my first $100K sales month in under two-and-a-half years from starting my online business.

The High-Ticket Method® *consists of six steps:*

- Psychology
- Perception
- POWER Offers
- Personalised Experiences
- Proven Results
- Premium Sales Strategies

I know how critical mastering high-ticket client attraction and sales are for your business and its impact on your success. I'll give you the exact steps I took to build the life and business of my wildest dreams by mastering high-ticket sales, so you can too…ethically.

Before we start, I need to get one thing off my proverbial chest: High-ticket sales do **not** mean simply adding another zero to the end of your price. If you think this book will deliver some get-rich-quick or Ponzi scheme, you'll be deeply disappointed and, frankly, you're in the wrong place.

There's another misconception I need to clear up before we dive in. I have nothing against low or mid-ticket offers or the clients who buy them, nor do I suggest you eradicate them from your business. While I believe that high-ticket, premium buyers are emotionally invested and ready to put in the work for life-changing results — great for your clients, your reputation and your business — I acknowledge that many clients buying low or mid-ticket offers are equally invested in achieving transformative results. So, while I love high-ticket sales, this isn't about excluding lower-ticket offers. There is a strategic place for them in every business. I hope that clears things up.

So, what makes a high-ticket client? A high-ticket client is someone who invests in premium offers from an expert, coach, mentor, consultant or service provider. Throughout this book, you'll see me use terms like 'high-ticket client', 'premium client', 'premium buyer' and 'high-calibre client' interchangeably — they all essentially mean the same thing.

High-ticket clients have specific characteristics that set them apart. The key one is that they either have or are able to find the financial resources to invest in higher ticket offers. Because high-ticket clients are paying above the industry average, they aren't just financially invested, they're emotionally invested too. This means they're ready to put in the work to achieve the results and ROI they desire through working with you.

These clients are often easier to work with and get results for because by needing fewer clients to meet your business and income goals, you can dedicate more time and resources to supporting them. This naturally elevates their results and as a by-product, enhances your reputation.

Another critical point you need to know is that, unlike the clients who generally invest in lower or mid-ticket offers, high-ticket clients will keep investing in your high-ticket offers even during economic downturns or a cost-of-living crisis, such as the one we're in as I write this. This means more stability, sustainability, security and scalability for your business.

Right now, I can almost hear you asking, *"So, Tania, what exactly makes a high-ticket offer?"*. I'm really glad you asked because this is a big one. We'll dive into an entire chapter on this later when I'll break down the ten essential elements that make your high-ticket offer irresistible to premium clients, but for now, you just need to know that a high-ticket offer is an offer, service, product, experience or container that is priced above the industry average. In the online space, we're talking thousands and multiple thousands, instead of hundreds. I hope that clears this one up for now!

Now, let's dive into the first game-changing mindset shift that will show you why converting high-ticket clients (or more high-ticket clients) is the missing piece in your strategy to skyrocket your impact and income.

It takes as much time and effort to create, launch and sell a high-ticket offer as it does a low or mid-ticket offer. The difference is that by mastering high-ticket sales, you'll maximise your return on investment (ROI) for your time and be paid more for each minute you spend in your business. Sounds good, right?

In business, you have two choices when it comes to where you want to operate. You can focus on selling lower ticket offers, which means you'll need to sell many of them to hit your revenue targets. This model requires volume. For example, let's say your monthly revenue goal is £20K. With a £1K product, you'd need to sell twenty of them each month to hit your goal.

Now, using the upper limit of the average audience-to-buyer conversion rate of 3%, to sell those two offers and hit your £20K monthly target, you'd need an audience size of around 666 people. If your conversion rate is closer to the lower end of the average audience-to-buyer conversion rate, for example, nearer 1%, you'll need an even larger audience. And if £20K per month is your consistent monthly goal, you'll need to continue growing your audience significantly each month just to sustain that target.

However, when you step into what I like to call *the arena of one*, you focus on creating stand-out, irresistible high-ticket offers that your ideal high-ticket clients can't refuse. In this scenario, if you have a £10K offer, you only need to sell two of them each month to hit your £20K revenue goal. Sticking with the 3% audience-to-conversion rate, you'd only need an engaged audience size of around sixty-six people. This means fewer clients, less audience growth needed and ultimately, less work on attracting multiple new clients to hit your monthly revenue goal.

Not only does this approach reduce the number of clients you need to hit your revenue goals but it also reduces your workload. With fewer clients to manage, you get to invest more in your existing clients. You free up more of your time, enabling you to achieve your financial goals without compromising your time or freedom.

My clients and I choose to operate in *the arena of one* all day long, focusing on attracting high-ticket clients so we can get paid more for the work that we love without multiplying our workload. I sincerely hope you'll be joining us!

THE MILLION DOLLAR QUESTION

I can't count the number of conversations I've had with entrepreneurs who tell me they're struggling to attract consistent high-ticket clients into their businesses. The thing is, when I ask the million-dollar question, *"What high-ticket offer(s) are you actively selling?"*, the answer is often *"none"*.

If you don't have a high-ticket offer and aren't actively promoting it to the right audience, you won't get high-ticket sales. You won't elevate your impact or income. It's that simple.

The most common reason experts and entrepreneurs aren't attracting high-ticket clients comes down to mindset. They either don't feel qualified, experienced or authoritative enough, or they're afraid that no one will buy their offers if they raise their prices.

The key here is that once you convert one high-ticket client, your courage, confidence and conviction skyrocket — and with that, so does your ability to take action and attract even more high-ticket clients. Mastering your mindset and psychology around money, pricing, converting and serving high-ticket clients is crucial for consistent high-ticket sales success, which is why Pillar One in *The High-Ticket Method*® is entirely dedicated to both your psychology and that of your ideal high-ticket client. We'll dive deep into this early on in the book because understanding and mastering this mindset is the foundation for everything that follows.

Mastering high-ticket client attraction is the one strategy that will skyrocket your impact, income and ultimately, your entire business. I can guarantee that if you're not yet consistently attracting and converting high-ticket clients and you're not hitting the revenue targets you desire, you're leaving hundreds of thousands of pounds (or dollars for our friends across the pond) on the table.

If this sounds like you, I promise that mastering high-ticket client attraction and sales is the missing piece in your business strategy. It's time to fill in that missing piece by adding a system that consistently attracts high-ticket clients — and that's exactly where this book comes in.

You're probably feeling much as I did just a few years ago, before I had my 'high-ticket epiphany'. I know how brilliant you are at your work and how you love what you do, but I also know that you'd love to get paid more for the work that you love, without multiplying your workload.

Right now, you're attracting good clients and making good money, but it's leaving you feeling exhausted and overworked.

The business you built for more freedom and time with your family and kids is having a huge impact on your family and personal life. Yes, you're making more money than you ever did in your previous job or career, but you're ready for so much more… and without sacrificing the very reasons you started this business in the first place.

Like me, you want quality, uncompromised time with your family and children. You want to take time off work without worrying that your income will drop as a result. You want the freedom to indulge now and again without having to worry about your bank balance. And of course, you want to give back to those who've always supported you — the ones who've always had your back, even when your business was nothing more than just an idea in your mind.

While you're currently attracting good clients who are ready to pay your existing fees, you're hungry to attract higher-paying, faster-moving clients who are ready and willing to invest in your higher rates which you know are ethically justifiable.

For you, this means attracting clients who are ready to take action without compromising your values by dropping your prices to accommodate clients who are no longer aligned with you. You want to move away from having to persuade clients to invest in you. You're ready to start attracting the higher-ticket clients with whom you feel aligned and who are ready and willing to invest in your highest-ticket offers yet. The thought of working with these higher-calibre clients excites you because you know you won't need to be pouring your heart and soul into them hiring you. It's already done.

Rest assured, this book will uncover everything you need to know, leaving no stone unturned in helping you attract and convert more high-ticket clients into your business for the impact and income you desire.

THE HIGH-TICKET METHOD® IS THE SOLUTION

The key to skyrocketing your impact and income is mastering high-ticket sales done ethically, and that's exactly what this book will help you achieve. I'll take you through *The High-Ticket Method*®, step-by-step.

This isn't just another book about raising your prices, hard sales tactics or 'bro marketing' — let's face it, there are enough of those out there to wallpaper the whole of Britain! So, if you're looking for a 'bro marketing' approach, this isn't the book for you. Instead, this book will be your guide to walk you through the science and strategy of attracting high-ticket clients, so you can get paid more for the work that you love whilst living your ultimate dream freedom lifestyle by design.

Using the proven six-step system outlined in *The High-Ticket Method*®, you'll learn ethical strategies that will elevate your impact and income while allowing you to operate with integrity, ensuring you can sleep soundly at night.

WHY THIS IS IMPORTANT

I'm no longer here for what society dictates I 'should' be doing. After more than thirty-five years of playing the 'good girl' — studying hard, getting into medical school and qualifying as a doctor and consultant radiologist — I still found myself feeling stuck, not knowing what I was supposed to do with my life. I was missing special family time and celebrations. Whilst on paper everything looked 'perfect', I felt like I was trapped inside the life and career of someone else, not one that was meant for me. The one thing I did know was that I was born to help others.

For the first thirty-five years of my life, I believed that the way I was born to help others was by helping them improve their health as a doctor. But as I progressed through my medical career, I realised I was deeply unhappy with the stress, long hours, missed special family occasions and genuine lack of freedom due to my relentless forty-plus-hour work weeks, including frequent twenty-four-hour weekend shifts.

I was handcuffed to the system. I remember coming home and falling into my husband's arms. I was desperate. I had very little of myself left to give because I was giving to everyone else. I felt so unfulfilled, trapped in a monotonous, never-ending rat race. I knew something had to change.

That's when it dawned on me: the way I was meant to help others was to help them create the lives and businesses of their wildest dreams — helping them to step out of the ordinary and into the extraordinary in terms of the impact they have and the crazy, illogical amounts of money they can make by building the business of their dreams.

I started in the online space with no clue what I was doing... and I struggled. My journey began as a property mentor, as I had built up a small property portfolio. Early on, I followed what I thought I was supposed to do with my prices and offers: starting with low prices and gradually working up to higher ticket offers. I sold £150 offers and at one point, my private, one-to-one mentoring was £1500 for three months. But this strategy meant I'd have to grow a huge audience and I'd have to sell lots of lower ticket offers to reach the financial goals, something I knew would take a long time. It was a high-volume strategy, relying on a constant influx of clients and a high volume of sales to achieve my ambitious money and business goals.

Meanwhile, I watched others in my industry achieving multi-five-figure and six-figure months. I couldn't shake the feeling that there was a secret strategy that they were all in on that I didn't know about. Despite my hard graft, I still wasn't achieving the consistent high-income months I desired, and attracting high-paying, high-ticket clients was far from my reality.

I quickly realised that my strategy of selling a multitude of low- and mid-ticket offers and trying to grow a massive audience just wasn't going to get me to my big, audacious money goals quickly or sustainably. Then it hit me: I was doing it all wrong.

Instead of trying to sell everything to everyone, I discovered that the key to reaching my consistent high-income goals fast was to focus on selling the right high-ticket offers to the right premium-paying clients. This shift meant being selective with the offers I created and the clients I was selling to.

This was my 'high ticket epiphany' — the turning point in my online career where I shifted my focus to selling primarily high-ticket offers, priced at least three times above the industry average, in a justifiable and ethical manner. I concentrated on delivering transformational offers and online programmes without needing a massive audience, a large team or costly ads.

This approach allowed me to achieve my first £30K launch with a Facebook group of fewer than 600 people and just one other person on my team. It's also the reason I achieved my first £100K sales month in under three years. It's also one of the key things that enabled me to emigrate with my young family from the UK to Ibiza in 2021 to pursue the true freedom fueled lifestyle by design I wanted for so long.

By combining my expertise in positive psychology and business strategy, I've developed my proven six-step strategy and science-backed system, *The High-Ticket Method*®. This is the exact system I guide my close proximity clients through and it's exactly what I'll be uncovering for you, step-by-step, throughout this book.

When it comes to high-ticket client attraction and sales, I know exactly what works and what doesn't. And by reading this book and implementing what we cover together, you will too.

No more settling for clients who don't light you up or who aren't fully committed to achieving great results. No more having to convince or persuade clients to buy. And definitely no more accepting an income below what you know your work is worth.

This book is your key to making more of the money you deserve, without compromising your most valuable asset: your time.

WHAT YOU CAN EXPECT FROM THIS BOOK

Now, here's my guarantee to you. If you digest and implement everything we cover in this book, I promise to shatter any misconceptions you have around pricing, serving higher calibre clients and making illogical amounts money. I'll show you how consistently converting your ideal, high-paying clients can become your reality sooner than you think.

But it doesn't stop there. Your impact and income will soar as a direct result of the strategies we explore together, step-by-step, through *The High-Ticket Method*®.

THE PROOF IS IN THE PUDDING. TRUST ME, I'M A DOCTOR

You might be thinking that high-ticket clients aren't for you, either because you don't have a big enough audience, you don't believe high-ticket clients are in your audience, you feel you're not experienced enough or you simply can't ever imagine someone paying you thousands (let alone tens of thousands) to work with you.

Throughout this book, I will bust these myths and tackle your concerns head-on. By the end, I guarantee you'll have everything you need to make converting more high-ticket clients your new baseline and reality. I'll also share real examples of clients I've worked with, who've implemented *The High-Ticket Method*® and achieved game-changing, tangible results. For transparency, whilst all examples and results are real and based on true client experiences, I won't be revealing specific client names or identifiers for confidentiality reasons.

My clients are transitioning from thinking and playing small to boldly owning their authority as the go-to expert for high-ticket clients and achieving their highest multi-five-figure launches and consistent multi-five-figure cash months. As an example, they've gone from struggling to sell their lower ticket offers to doubling their rates and having a flood of their highest-paying clients yet. Throughout this book, I'll walk you through every step of my results-driven system, *The High-Ticket Method*®, so you can achieve similar results too. There's just one thing I need you to remember: If they can, so can you.

THE IMPACT THIS BOOK WILL HAVE

Imagine yourself, six or twelve months from now, with your business consistently bringing in high-paying, fast-moving clients every single month. Picture how that will feel — not just for you but for your family and those who depend on you. Not only will it mean more income each month, but it will also mean more stability, sustainability and security for your business and your loved ones. This is about embodying the very reason you started your business in the first place: to spend more quality time with your family and loved ones and to live your ultimate freedom lifestyle by design, without compromise. To enjoy the things you love on your terms, working when you want, free from the stress of constantly chasing clients or scrambling to bring in more money… because with the right system in place, it's already done.

It also means that your business becomes even more exciting, because not only are you consistently bringing in more income, but you're also working with the higher-caliber invested clients who light you up. These are the clients who are ready to do the work with you for big, transformational results — clients who don't need you to spend hours convincing or persuading them to invest or do the work; they already know that you're the high-ticket expert for them. Business becomes fun and dynamic, and when Monday morning rolls around, you're ready to jump out of bed and throw yourself into the life and business that you've intentionally built by design.

This is what high-ticket sales and clients mean for my clients and for me, and I'm going to show you exactly how this can become your reality, too.

EXACTLY WHAT YOU'LL LEARN IN THIS BOOK

High-ticket client attraction and sales start with mindset and extend to mastering everything from fully understanding your ideal premium client's psychology to crafting copy that turns your free content into paying high-ticket clients. You need to elevate your brand and how your audience perceives you because, in their mind, perception equals reality. It's about embracing the mindset of creating an offer they simply can't refuse. This is where I'll guide you through my POWER offer framework, revealing the key ingredients for an irresistible high-ticket offer that consistently brings in premium clients.

It's not just about creating offers, though. It's about crafting offers that stand out from the crowd, ones your ideal premium buyers simply cannot say no to. It requires creating, planning and delivering high-ticket, personalised experiences that premium buyers are willing to invest in. Building your reputation as the go-to expert who consistently delivers results is essential, and we'll dive into my 'Clients-and-Cash-on-Repeat' system to do exactly that.

Finally, you'll need to master premium sales strategies that work specifically for high-ticket buyers. These aren't the same sales strategies that everyone is using on the internet for converting low- and mid-ticket buyers — they don't all work for premium clients. I'll be teaching you the proven high-ticket sales strategies that convert premium buyers into long-term clients for your business.

As you can see, *The High-Ticket Method*® offers a full 360-degree approach to attracting and converting high-ticket clients. It's not just about *"sell, sell, sell"* for the sake of making money. This is a comprehensive, step-by-step system that shows you exactly how to get paid more for the work you love, ethically and with a client-centric approach. You'll learn how to position yourself as a trusted and in-demand expert, build long-lasting client relationships and brand advocates and deliver transformational results — all while maintaining integrity and doing what lights you up.

IT'S TIME TO GET STARTED

This book is my life's work, crafted to help you achieve the elevated impact and income you desire in your business.

You're ready for more high-ticket clients. You're ready to elevate both your impact and income for your *ultimate* freedom lifestyle by design. You're ready to turn the page and unlock the power of *The High-Ticket Method*®.

Tania

ONE
ELEVATE YOUR MINDSET TO ATTRACT HIGH-TICKET CLIENTS

At this stage, you might feel what I call the *"mindset monkeys"* creeping in, whispering doubts like *"High-ticket clients aren't for you"*, or *"Maybe those multi-five and six-figure months won't ever become your reality"*. They might say that you aren't good enough to charge high-ticket prices, that you can't serve high-ticket clients, that you've not been in business long enough, that you can't charge high-ticket prices for what you do, or that you don't even have high-ticket clients in your audience. Right now, you may not be able to imagine someone ever paying you five, multi-five or even six figures to work with you.

I want you to know that this is normal, but with love, these thoughts are wrong.

For context, I know people who get paid £100K a year for their one-to-one packages. Let that sink in. **If they can, you can too.**

We're going to dive straight into the psychology behind these doubts. As an academic and doctor, I need as much as possible of what I teach to be backed by evidence, so let's explore this... I promise to keep it simple.

The reason these thoughts surface is that your subconscious mind is trying to keep you safe. It controls 95% of your thoughts, emotions and actions without you even realising it. This powerful part of your mind is shaped by your early experiences, particularly between the ages of zero and seven, when much of it was formed and cemented under the influence of those who had the greatest impact on you then, likely your parents or guardians. Your subconscious wants to keep you within your comfort zone — the periphery of what I call *"your leading edge"* — within which, everything feels safe and familiar. It's like your favourite armchair: cosy, comforting and easy to stay in. But ultimately, nothing new like bigger results, higher-paying clients or more money, happens in that chair.

So, here's the key: When you start thinking about attracting high-ticket clients and elevating your income, the first thing your subconscious will throw at you is fear. Fear of failure, fear of not being good enough or fear of what others will think. I tell my clients all the time and now I'm telling you: Whenever you commit to something new, fear will always be the first thing that greets you.

The fear is a sign **you're on the right path.**

The only difference between where you are now and where the experts you see as successful are — the ones who consistently attract high-ticket clients and earn more — is that they've learned to push past their comfort zones. They've grown comfortable with being uncomfortable. They've committed to *"doing the thing"* despite the fear and as a by-product, they get the results.

CHECK YOUR MONEY MINDSET

At this point, it's important to talk about money mindset. If you're struggling with thoughts of not being good enough to serve high-ticket clients, or feeling unworthy of making extraordinary money, you're not alone. Let me share a bit of my story to show you that even those of us who now attract high-ticket clients didn't always have it figured out.

I can't think of a better time in this book than now to give you an insight into my background, where I've come from and what a flaky money mindset I've carried around with me for more than thirty-five years, which, by the way, is still a work in progress which will never be complete.

I come from what my mum used to call *"mixed heritage"*, half Iraqi, half Essex (for anyone from outside the UK, Essex is a county in the UK). If you want to confuse a child about who they are, try mixing strict Middle Eastern values with the laid-back culture of Essex, all while growing up in the UK. It's a recipe for confusion on many levels but that's a story for another day.

My money mindset was shaped by my parents. The money story I've carried with me for thirty-five years can only be described as the heaviest luggage you could imagine and if I'm completely honest, was completely messed up. My wonderful dad has lived in council housing for most of his life since emigrating to the UK. He's one of six children and I've always seen his siblings as uber-successful. They are or were all doctors, with thriving practices and businesses. My dad was different. He decided that medicine wasn't for him and chose a different path in engineering. I've always felt like we were the 'poorest' in the family. We didn't have the luxuries that my uncles, aunts and cousins had, like flashy cars, aeroplanes and huge houses. This was the norm for them but not for us.

At any family gatherings, I always felt like the poor kid at the table and for whatever reason, I felt like I was looked down on and that I didn't belong. Looking back, I believe that this wasn't actually true, rather it was a belief created in my mind. But it's how I felt for most of my life. Growing up, there was no comparison to the expansive homes in which my uncles, aunts and cousins lived and and my reality.

To protect me, my dad's belief was always that money should be saved, not spent. He drilled into me that credit cards were a sin and borrowing was out of the question. It's easy to see now where this came from — a lack mindset due to his lack of income or money. I also see that this was, and still is, his way of caring for and protecting me. Out of his true love and dedication to me, he didn't ever want me to end up without much money, like him which I completely understand. If you're reading this Dad, thank you for your ever-lasting love and protection. I understand that everything you've done and continue to do for me has always and undoubtedly been with my best interests at heart. I love you so much, more than words could ever say. I wouldn't be here, doing what I do now and writing this book, if it wasn't for you.

My mum, on the other hand, bought a 17.5-acre estate when I was around twelve years old, but literally sank every last penny she had and maxed out her credit cards to maintain it, leaving us with nothing much to enjoy. Neither of my parents was great with money. Growing up, one barely had any and the other spent it without a plan, so, as you can imagine, not only was my identity of who I was being half Middle Eastern and half 'Essex' very confusing, but so too was my mindset and money story for at least thirty-five years of my life, which is when I first discovered personal development.

For most of my life, I carried around a deeply ingrained identity of being *"the poor kid"*. When I spent time with my wealthy relatives, I felt out of place and like I was different to them because we didn't have the money they did. Because of this, for most of my life, I never thought I was worthy of sitting at the same table as millionaires or billionaires. I still have work to do on this because as I always say with transparency, this work will always be a work in progress.

Until recently, I was never good at saving or investing money. I spent it as fast as I received it, thinking life was all about having a good time. I wasn't programmed to save, invest or think long-term when it came to money, because I simply wasn't aware of what money meant and had no idea on how to use or invest it. My mindset around money was completely off and I didn't even realise it. Unfortunately, the world of personal development didn't exist for me at that time.

If I saw a young guy driving a Porsche, I'd automatically assume he was a drug dealer. Ridiculous, right? It's embarrassing to admit, but I need to be honest with you. I had a story about money that didn't serve me and maybe you do too. If you do, you are not alone. Most of us have some form of limiting belief or unhealthy relationship with money. If someone claims they've never had a money mindset issue they're either not being honest or they've had everything handed to them on a plate.

THE WAKE-UP CALL

Until 2011, I took so much in my life for granted. Then, my entire world changed in an instant.

It was my wedding day, the 24th of October 2011. My mum was there, of course, but I noticed she wasn't eating. Every bite she took seemed to get stuck in her throat. I remember her excusing herself to the bathroom because she wasn't feeling great, and food seemed to be getting stuck, but I never could have imagined what was happening inside her body. We had no idea what was coming – news that would shatter everything in my life.

In November 2011, my beautiful mum Estelle was diagnosed with oesophageal cancer.

It was November the 11th, at 11:11 a.m. I'll never forget that moment — the surreal, gut-wrenching timing of it all. My mum was only fifty-six years old, but the cancer had already reached a point where it was too late. It was the kind that hides quietly until there's no turning back. Until it's too late.

That day changed me forever.

It's hard to put into words how that kind of shock shifts everything — your priorities, your perspective, your beliefs. At that moment, money meant nothing, but it also meant everything. I knew that how I had been living had to change. I had to change. My story about money, my story about life... everything was about to evolve.

Mum's diagnosis came out of nowhere. She had always been healthy, or so I thought. When she was diagnosed, it hit me like a freight train. She was a psychology teacher at the local senior school and I remember her telling me how much she wanted to hand in her notice to embrace the freedom-fuelled lifestyle she'd dreamt of for years and go travelling — South America was where she dreamed of starting. She wanted to immerse herself in new cultures and learn new languages and not be shackled to a mortgage and her 'traditional' life that no-longer fulfilled her. Travel was her passion. She had such vivid dreams of freedom, of leaving behind the grind of her nine-to-five and escaping the disrespectful kids at school that weighed heavily on her. She deserved more than that. Her dream was so close. She'd had enough and was on the verge of handing in her notice to embrace this new chapter, a life of adventure and exploration.

But in an instant, it was all stripped away from her.

Everything changed overnight. Instead of planning her travels, she was thrust into an exhausting routine of oesophageal-gastric surgery, chemotherapy, radiotherapy and countless doctor's appointments. I spent every weekend travelling down from London, where I was working as a doctor, to Devon to be with her and take her to appointments.

At first, we held onto hope. We wanted so badly to believe she would pull through. I'll never forget the day she was diagnosed. That night, we went to a local pub to see our close friend Ron's band play. I remember the moment so vividly. Ron started playing Bob Marley's *"Don't Worry."*

I was overwhelmed with emotion. There we were, in this surreal space between fear and hope. As Ron sang *"Don't worry,"* I looked her straight in the eyes, singing the words back to her. I wanted her to know that I believed everything would be okay. I wanted to reassure her, even when my own heart was breaking.

Mum's strength amazed me. Even after her gastrointestinal surgeon told her she was his fastest patient to recover from such extensive gastro-oesophageal surgery, she wore that achievement like a badge of honour. I remember her hope so vividly – cycling together through the countryside in North Devon with a pouch of chemotherapy attached to her. She called it her *"little army,"* always fighting, always working to rid her of this awful disease.

Every time I visited her, we'd sit together on Saturday nights, the TV on, but I wasn't watching. My eyes were on her, absorbing her presence, holding onto each moment. I was so deeply grateful for every breath, every smile and every second we had together. But beneath that gratitude was a gnawing fear — the terror of losing her, of her being ripped away from me. It felt like a ticking time bomb. My anxiety was constant and I couldn't escape the dread of potentially losing her.

Then, one year and one month after her diagnosis, my worst fear came true. On December the 15th, 2012, at home in Devon, she passed away in my arms. She was my best friend. I was her only child and at that moment, I felt completely and utterly lost.

Losing mum at Christmas, as an only child, was the most terrifying and heartbreaking experience of my life. But somewhere in that grief, I also found the biggest lesson: life is not a rehearsal. Her death shook me to my core and it continues to test me every single day. We were best friends and I honestly believe no one had the kind of mother-daughter bond we shared. We were inseparable. Losing her ripped my world apart.

But in that pain, a realisation struck me: life is too short to play small, too fragile not to chase after our dreams. Mum's passing taught me that life isn't guaranteed and that none of us know how much time we have. And, though I'm ashamed to admit it, I took so much for granted before then.

Somehow, through my grief, I found a strength I didn't know existed. It was as though Mum was still by my side, guiding me and watching over me. Her loss fueled a fire in me. If I could survive losing her, my best friend and my anchor, then I could survive anything. I made a vow that I wouldn't just live for myself anymore; I would live for both of us. I committed to creating a life of freedom, one she so desperately wanted but sadly never got the chance to experience.

That's when everything changed. Losing her forced me to completely reevaluate my life. A few years later, I left behind my career as a doctor, which was driving me to burnout, depression and exhaustion. I chose freedom, purpose and a life filled with opportunity.

This indescribable loss, coupled with becoming a mother myself, transformed me. I now live with an unwavering commitment to never settle for anything less than what I truly desire. Being a mother to my two beautiful daughters drives me every day. I want to be their role model, to show them that they can create their ultimate freedom lifestyle by design beyond their wildest dreams. To be that example, I had to let go of my chronic small thinking and embrace the discomfort and challenge of activating the limitless potential within me. It was time for me to start feeling worthy of sitting at the same table as millionaires and billionaires.

This transformation required me to completely rewire my deeply ingrained and, frankly, unhealthy money mindset. I had to go all in on building businesses that fueled my freedom, allowing me to walk away from my long-standing job as an NHS doctor, having started to build a successful property business. It meant shifting my focus in my online business toward high-ticket sales, intentionally attracting premium clients who were ready to invest at higher levels. I knew that this was the fastest path to creating the income and impact I desired, along with the choice to live my ultimate freedom-based life on my own terms.

Now, because of this shift, I regularly attract high-ticket clients and I've been able to generate multi-five and even six figures in sales in a single month. I'm able to live my dream freedom fueled lifestyle by design with my family in Ibiza. Even writing that down feels surreal because just a few years ago it seemed like an impossible dream. But today, this is my reality and it's a direct result of the deep personal development work I've done, especially when it comes to my money mindset and mastering high-ticket sales.

I'm living proof that when you commit to transforming your beliefs about money and your worth, everything changes.

Thinking and playing big haven't always come naturally to me. For much of my life, I was a chronic small thinker. I remember back when I was a doctor, believing that if I could just reach a £100K salary by working extra hours privately on top of my NHS work, that would be the peak of my earning potential and I wouldn't be able to get beyond that. £100K felt like a huge amount of money and it still does, but I had no idea at the time that I could build a business that could generate far more than that in the online space. I truly believed that was my ceiling, unable to imagine anything beyond it. Looking back now, I realise that this was my financial thermostat holding me back — a reflection of the way I'd been programmed for over thirty-five years to think small and stay within certain limits, especially when it came to money. It stemmed from my deep-rooted belief that I wasn't worthy of sitting at the same table as millionaires and billionaires.

IT'S POSSIBLE FOR YOU TOO

I hope that by sharing my journey, complete with my struggles around mindset and money and my feelings of unworthiness in the presence of money and millionaires, I can reassure you that you are not alone. Your mindset, particularly your money mindset, plays a crucial role in your success in attracting premium-paying clients and making high-ticket sales your normality.

For most of my life, I put money on a pedestal, giving it a meaning that was way beyond what it really is. I let it control my self-worth and sense of value, thinking that the amount I earned somehow defined who I was. Can you relate? This misguided reverence for money meant that I equated my worth and value to what my bank balance was, instead of recognising my true inherent worth.

I was wrong. Money is just a tool—it represents an exchange of value that should empower us, not dictate our self-worth. It's not a measure of our value, abilities, impact, or potential. When I had this realisation, it changed everything for me. I came to understand that my true value comes from within, from the impact I make and the lives I touch.

I want you to know that if you've struggled with an unhealthy money story, you, too, can reclaim your power. It's time to redefine your relationship with money, to see it for what it is — a resource that can help amplify your impact, not a determinant of your worth. You are so much more than the numbers in your bank account and once you embrace this, the possibilities are endless.

The money story you've carried with you for most of your life doesn't have to dictate your future. You have the power to choose a new narrative, one that aligns with the impact and income you aspire to create in your life and business. Now is your moment to decide to become the go-to expert for premium-paying clients in your industry.

This requires a bold decision, one that can change everything. I promise you, if you commit to the strategies I share throughout this book, using *The High-Ticket Method*®, your transformation will be huge. The work that we will do together can significantly enhance your business, revenue, profit margins and, ultimately, your freedom and wealth.

I'll guide you through exactly what works and how to implement these strategies in the real world, empowering you to attract and convert premium paying clients consistently.

I know your mindset monkeys might be chattering away right now, whispering doubts from your subconscious mind that high-ticket clients aren't in your reach because you don't have a massive audience. You might be thinking, *"What if there aren't any high-ticket clients in my audience?"*

Let's set the record straight: while it's true that having an audience is essential for high-ticket sales, it's not about the size of that audience, it's about the quality. You don't need thousands of followers to attract your ideal premium-paying clients; you need a focused, engaged community that resonates with your message and sees you as the only choice to help solve their problems.

I remember launching my first high-ticket offer to a Facebook™ group of fewer than 600 people. That launch brought in an incredible £30K! How? I spoke directly to my ideal higher-ticket clients, understanding their needs, desires and pain points. The key isn't numbers; it's connection and how they perceive you to be the only solution to solving their problem.

So, if you're feeling stuck, remember this: you absolutely can attract high-ticket clients, even with a smaller audience. The secret lies in your approach and the value and energy you bring to the table. Get ready to refine your messaging and become known as the go-to expert for high-ticket clients in your niche, because high-ticket clients are ready and waiting for you to step up and claim your high-ticket expert identity so they can hire you to solve the problems only you can solve!

Understanding the role your subconscious mind plays in keeping you safe — and simultaneously limiting your potential — will be crucial in our next chapter. We will explore mindset hacks that will help you become the go-to expert for high-ticket clients in your niche so that consistent premium-paying clients become your reality too.

This book isn't just your step-by-step guide to mastering high-ticket client attraction and conversion; it's a roadmap to elevating your identity. There are high-ticket clients out there, ready and waiting to invest in you, some will already be part of your audience and network. But they're waiting for you to step into your identity as their go-to expert.

It's time to take up space in your industry, to show them why you are the expert they need, and to present your power offer as the essential bridge from where they are now, at point A, to where they want to be, at point B. Only then will your ideal premium-paying clients see you, hire you and pay you as their trusted go-to expert.

It's time to turn the page to multiply your impact and skyrocket your income potential by getting seen, hired and paid as the in-demand expert for premium-paying, high-ticket clients!

ACCESS YOUR EXCLUSIVE HIGH-TICKET MASTERY MINI-COURSE

To help you take the next step and deepen your learning with the work we've done in Chapter One and throughout the book, I've created something special just for you. As an exclusive offer for my book readers, you can access a **free mini-course,** packed full of additional resources to help you consolidate everything you've learned in this chapter.

Simply go to **bit.ly/Highticketmethodbookcourse** to access your Chapter One resources to further accelerate your high-ticket journey now!

TWO
ACTIVATE YOUR HIGH-TICKET IDENTITY

YOUR WAKE-UP CALL: WHY HIGH-TICKET CLIENTS ARE THE MISSING PIECE IN YOUR STRATEGY

As we dive deeper into ethical high-ticket sales, a fundamental mindset shift is necessary for you to start attracting consistent high-ticket clients. One of the philosophies I always encourage my clients to embody is: *"Who would I be, how would I show up and what would I deliver if my clients were paying me double, triple, even ten times what they're currently paying me?"* This question instantly shifts your energy, quality of content and how you show up in your business. Whether it's free value you offer or paid programmes, thinking from the perspective of commanding higher prices naturally elevates the value you deliver and the level of impact you create. The key here is to always lead from a place of service.

But here's the crux: if you're blending in with everyone else in your niche, taking the same actions, showing up like everyone else in your niche and launching the same offers, you'll get the same average results. You'll struggle to stand out in the crowded online space. There's a constant barrage of noise and distractions that easily pull audiences away and it's never going to get quieter. What will happen is that you keep adding to the noise, instead of standing out from it and becoming your own orchestra! Simply adding to the noise won't get you the extraordinary results you crave. But I want you to break out of this cycle. You deserve to make extraordinary money and create a lasting impact on your clients, and they deserve nothing less from you. This requires you to embrace and embody your high-ticket identity.

To step into this new identity, you first need to unlock your wealth psychology, which will help you fully embody your high-ticket identity. This is why your psychology is the first pillar of *The High-Ticket Method*®. It's crucial to break through your current money mindset and embrace a psychology that supports consistent high-ticket sales with ease.

CLIENT TRANSFORMATION

This kind of transformation is something I work on frequently with my clients. Many come to me feeling unworthy of charging high-ticket prices, unable to imagine anyone paying them the rates they really want to earn. One client in particular stands out. She was struggling to fill her high-ticket offer and her sales were inconsistent – she was experiencing the rollercoaster of sales that many refer to as feast or famine. She knew she was good at what she did but lacked the confidence and audacity to position herself as the go-to expert for high-ticket clients in her niche because she wasn't sure how to do it and had never charged high-ticket prices before.

Together, we tackled her limiting beliefs about being unworthy of higher prices and repositioned her as the only authority in her field. The results were dramatic: she doubled her prices and immediately began attracting her highest-paying clients to date. Her high-ticket offer filled faster than she could've imagined. She was genuinely stunned and excited that clients were now paying her double, effortlessly, and it actually felt easier for her to attract clients at this new level.

This shift led to her two biggest consecutive months in business. A few months in, she even told me words to the effect of, *"I can't believe how little I was charging before. I was selling myself so short. Even now, it feels like my pricing isn't high enough"*.

You see, this client had a deeply ingrained, limiting money story and lots of self-limiting beliefs which were holding her back from taking action and making much more money. Raising her prices definitely pushed her out of her comfort zone. Lots of mindset monkeys came up for her, which brought up feelings of anxiety and doubt and left her wondering whether it would really work for her. But it did. The good news for you is, if she can do it, coming from an unhealthy relationship with money and deep-rooted self-limiting beliefs, you absolutely can too. All she did was decide that enough was enough. She took action, got the right support and committed to the process that delivered those results.

And you can do the same.

⭐

But first, it's time for a wake-up call! I need you to understand why attracting consistent high-ticket clients is absolutely essential for skyrocketing your impact and income in your business. It's time to shift your mindset from thinking, *"It would be nice to convert more high-ticket clients,"* to realising, *"More high-ticket clients are the key to unleashing the explosive growth I want in my business!"* This shift isn't just a nice-to-have; it's your fast-track to the income, impact and success you want.

SO, WHY HIGH-TICKET CLIENTS?

Selling high-ticket offers enables you to invest more time and effort into each of your clients, leading to bigger results and returns on investment for your clients. You get to invest more in your clients and co-create better results with them without adding to your workload. If you know anything about me, you'll know I'm all about working smarter, not harder and attracting high-ticket sales ticks this box immediately.

When it comes to the economy, high-ticket clients are less negatively impacted by economic downturns in comparison to those who generally invest in low- and mid-ticket offers, allowing you to build a business to last which thrives regardless of any external economic conditions, therefore giving you more stability and security than one just built on low- and mid-ticket offers. What this means is high-ticket clients continue to pay for your services even during economic downturns. They also pay more per offer or service and therefore provide a higher revenue per client. This means that because you can generate more revenue, you can build wealth faster because you have more funds to invest in wealth-building strategies that multiply your money and build true, generational wealth, such as property investments, in my case.

There are even more advantages to converting high-ticket clients in your business. As we've already discussed, creating, launching and selling high-ticket offers requires the same time and effort as low or mid-ticket offers. By prioritising high-ticket sales, you instantly multiply your return on investment (ROI) on the time that you invest in your business. Plus, with fewer clients needed to hit your financial targets, you can dedicate more time and resources to each high-ticket client. This means you'll co-create better results without increasing your workload. Ultimately, you'll elevate your revenue and profit margins, allowing you to reach your financial goals faster. As you'll uncover later in this book, this triggers my 'Clients-and-Cash-on-Repeat' system, setting you on the path to effortlessly multiply your revenue in the simplest way.

It's important to note here that the term *"high-ticket offer"* or *"high-ticket sales"* varies from person to person. My definition of a high-ticket price starts at around the £5K mark and can go up to multi-five and six figures and beyond. Your definition and pricing may differ and that's perfectly fine.

MASTER YOUR PSYCHOLOGY FOR CONSISTENT HIGH-TICKET SALES

To attract premium-paying clients consistently, your job is to exude confidence in yourself and your offers. Your potential clients will sense your energy and confidence long before they hear your pitch. So, bearing this in mind, it's important that you eliminate any limiting beliefs around money, pricing and your value as an expert.

It's your job to commit to leading yourself first and becoming the go-to expert for high-ticket clients in your niche before anyone else sees you as such. Doing this requires you to let go of any fears of rejection, unworthiness or guilt around charging high prices. I see many entrepreneurs hold onto money blocks like this, leading them to underprice their offers, being hesitant when they come to pitch and even dropping their prices out of fear that no one will pay or that they'll lose potential clients to their cheaper competition.

Blocks like this lead to playing small, which will directly impact your income. But the good news is, it takes just one decision to break this cycle. The limiting beliefs and money stories you've carried with you don't have to define your future. You can decide just like I had to, that today is the day that you claim your position as the expert for high-ticket clients, to attract the impact, income and freedom you desire.

It takes one decision for you to create a new high-ticket offer and one decision for you to sell it. It also only takes one person to decide to buy that offer to become your next high-ticket client. Making quick, confident decisions is key to success, especially when it comes to attracting high-ticket clients. Every action you take, from creating a new high-ticket offer to launching and selling it, can open doors to new high-ticket clients. The only thing in the way of you attracting consistent high-ticket clients is you. So, it's time to stop deliberating over your decision-making because success comes to those who make decisions quickly and with conviction. Your next high-ticket clients are out there, so, let's go and find them.

IDENTIFYING AND CONFRONTING YOUR MONEY BLOCKS AND LIMITING BELIEFS

As you read this, you might notice your mindset monkeys surfacing in your thoughts. They might be whispering things like, *"Who am I to charge this much?"* or *"What if they don't see the value in me?"* These thoughts are completely normal when first venturing into the world of high-ticket sales, but they can be significant barriers to your growth if left unchecked. Acknowledge them! Recognising these blocks is the first step to dismantling their power over you.

Now, instead of letting those mindset blocks take control of you and your actions, I invite you to challenge them. Ask yourself: *"What evidence do I have that supports my value?"* Remind yourself of your unique skills, experiences and the transformative results you co-create with your clients. If you don't yet have the client results, focus on the results that you have gained for yourself. Embrace the belief that your expertise is not only valuable but necessary. The truth is, the right clients are out there, waiting for an expert like you to guide them, but they're waiting for you to show up first.

So, let's shift that mindset! When you fully believe in your worth and the impact of your offers, you will naturally attract premium clients who resonate with your energy and value. Your journey starts with a single decision: to believe in yourself and your ability to deliver exceptional value. But it needs to come from you first.

CRAFTING YOUR PATHWAY TO PREMIUM CLIENTS

I believe in doing things differently in the online space. Instead of following the conventional path of starting with low-ticket offers and gradually progressing to high-ticket ones, as many so-called *"online gurus"* suggest, I recommend implementing my three-step, *"One-to-More System"* (see the graphic representation below). This system provides a clear and obvious client pathway while elevating your Client Lifetime Value (CLV), which measures the total amount of money a client spends in your business whilst engaging with and investing in your services.

THE ONE TO MORE SYSTEM

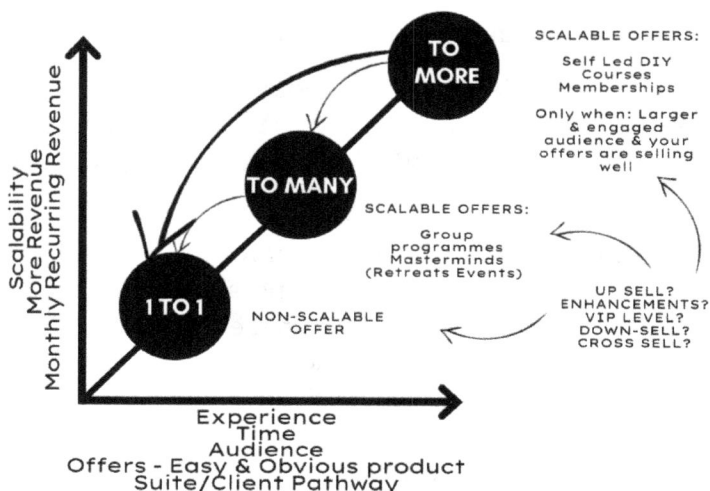

THE ONE-TO-MORE SYSTEM

In step one of the *"One-to-More"* system, we kick things off by launching a key, signature high-ticket offer, such as one-to-one mentoring, VIP days or experiences. This gives clients close proximity to you and allows you to build your expertise, collect your social proof and refine your unique signature system, just like the one I'm guiding you through in this book, *The High-Ticket Method*®.

As you build momentum through client results, experience and audience growth, we move to step two: adding mid- to high-ticket offers delivered in a group setting. Examples include masterminds and group programmes. These scalable offers are crucial for growing your business because there's no limit on the number of participants, which therefore means unlimited revenue potential. Plus, since you're training a group rather than individual clients, your delivery time remains consistent and doesn't go up in these containers. This stage is effective only when you've engaged an audience that resonates with you, your brand and your message.

Finally, in stage three, we incorporate more scalable, lower-ticket offers like memberships and DIY courses, where multiple participants can join any offer but where access to you privately isn't offered or is extremely limited.

Having this clear client pathway serves three key objectives: First, it provides a range of experiences and offers for clients, based on where they currently are in their journey and budget. Secondly, you have the next obvious step in terms of offer, for your clients to join once they finish the existing offer they're in, so it elevates your Client Lifetime Value (CLV) — the monetary value each client brings to your business during their time with you. Thirdly, by focusing on high-ticket offers first and foremost, you'll require fewer clients to achieve the impact and income you desire. Having these three tiers to your offers also means that you stop leaving thousands of unclaimed sales on the table because you have something for everyone.

This three-step strategy allows you to build and maintain higher revenue while serving a smaller number of clients, enabling you to optimise your time invested in your business and your client results. We'll dive deeper into it later on in the book.

YOU'RE NOT EXPENSIVE; YOU'RE PRICELESS. START ACTING LIKE IT

> "YOU'RE NOT EXPENSIVE; YOU'RE PRICELESS. START ACTING LIKE IT."
>
> — TANIA KING-MOHAMMAD

This is where my work can sometimes get controversial. I advise pricing all levels of your offers above the industry average, but this should only be achieved by adding extra value to your offers, products or services, so that they truly stand out in your industry in terms of the value and transformation created – as I've already stated, high-ticket sales are not about just adding a zero onto your price. I'll show you exactly how to do this and how to create your next irresistible high-ticket offer in the upcoming chapter all about power offers.

Let's get one thing straight: I practice what I preach. Throughout my online business journey, I've faced the critics and naysayers who insisted that to reach my financial goals, I needed to cut my prices. They doubted my high-ticket offers, claiming they wouldn't sell because my rates were above industry standards. I, too, questioned myself at times. There were moments when it didn't feel comfortable to stand firm in my pricing. The doubts crept in, making me wonder if I was on the right path and making me question if I would hit my goals. But I stood my ground. Why? Because I wholeheartedly believe in the value and transformation I deliver to my clients. The results we achieve together speak volumes. The work I do literally changes lives.

I constantly seek out gaps in the market where I can elevate my offers, infusing them with added value that cuts through the noise in my niche. I don't just talk the talk; I walk the walk. Embracing my high-ticket identity has been crucial to be able to achieve my results to date. I know that I'm the expert in my niche, I know exactly who my offers are for, and I'm confident that my ideal high-ticket clients are out there, ready to invest. It's that straightforward. This is exactly where I want you to be after reading this book.

I apply the very strategies I'm sharing with you in this book. These exact strategies are what propelled me to my first £100K launch in under two-and-a-half years of building my online business, so, trust me when I say this works, even if it feels uncomfortable at times. You're not alone in your doubts; it's all part of the journey.

REWIRING YOUR NEGATIVE MONEY BELIEFS: EXERCISE

Your thoughts and beliefs shape your reality, which is why rewiring any negative money beliefs that you may have now is essential for you to start attracting consistent high-ticket clients for the impact and income that you desire. One powerful exercise to begin this process is called 'reframing'. Here's how it works: Identify a negative money belief you currently hold, write it down and then replace it with the polar opposite, empowering belief, which I also want you to write down.

For example:

- Negative belief: *"I'll never attract £20K clients."*
- Reframed belief: *"I am open to unlimited £20K clients who choose and commit to working with me with simplicity and ease."*

Alongside reframing, I recommend practising daily affirmations and money mantras. For instance, try starting with gratitude:

"I am grateful for the exciting high-ticket clients I already have." Then, use present-tense statements like: *"I consistently attract £20K clients effortlessly."* Then bring positive emotions into your affirmations such as *"I feel worthy of and excited by working with clients who are ready to pay me £20K."* Finally, tie these affirmations to specific financial goals: *"I attract [specific amount] easily because I am the go-to expert for high-ticket clients who hire and pay me with ease."*

These exercises are important because, with practice, they start to reprogram your subconscious mind and create thoughts, beliefs and actions which serve you and the results you want to achieve, especially when you make them specific and connect them to your emotions. The more specific and emotionally charged your affirmations and mantras, the more impactful they will be.

Importantly though, rewiring your subconscious mind using practices like this is a process that requires consistency. Your subconscious loves repetition. It's like a muscle; the more you train it, the bigger and easier it is to get results. So, I'm afraid to say that if you picked up this book expecting to practice these exercises once and gain an immediate result, it won't happen and you'll be hugely disappointed. However, the more you practice exercises like reframing and affirmations, the more these positive beliefs will become second nature to you. Over time, these new thoughts will start to replace any limiting beliefs which you do have, allowing you to step into your role as the high-ticket expert who gets seen, hired and paid the high-ticket amounts which you desire.

You can do this with any money block or self-limiting belief you have to turn them into thoughts and beliefs that serve you and the impact and income you want to make with high-ticket clients with practice and consistency.

THE ONLY PERMISSION SLIP YOU NEED IS THE ONE YOU WRITE YOURSELF

Attracting high-ticket clients consistently starts with adopting a wealth mindset that leads from a place of abundance rather than a place of scarcity. Your job is to lead from a belief that high-paying clients are already within your reach. It's already done.

Cultivating a strong wealth mindset is vital when it comes to attracting consistent, high-paying clients and will shape everything that you do in your business. It will not only impact your marketing and sales approach but also your willingness to take fast and calculated risks, embrace challenges, achieve financial breakthroughs and show up as the expert your ideal, premium-paying clients need. With this mindset, you'll be equipped to overcome any limiting beliefs, embrace new opportunities for growth and lead with the confidence you need to become the expert who is seen, hired and paid as the in-demand expert for high-paying clients. Ultimately, it'll support you in building the resilience and innovation you need in business, which are key factors to attract the high-paying premium clients you want.

However, if, in your business to date, you've not quite believed or realised that high-paying clients can be your consistent reality, this is the reason you've not yet attracted the high-paying clients you want. It's time for a perception shift. You need to believe and perceive that it's possible first before they will come. It's like flicking a switch; the moment you decide to stand out from the noise and become the only choice for high-ticket clients in your industry, everything changes. You lead first and the clients will follow.

> "STOP WAITING FOR PERMISSION TO TAKE ACTION. THE ONLY PERMISSION SLIP YOU NEED IS THE ONE YOU WRITE YOURSELF."
>
> — TANIA KING-MOHAMMAD

Now, you might be thinking, *"This all sounds great Tania, but how do I actually cultivate and, more importantly, maintain a wealth mindset?"* Let me share six key principles that I practice and teach to help you fully embody and sustain a wealth mindset. You can start applying them right away. At first, they might feel awkward or uncomfortable, but as you now understand, the more you practice, the more natural they become and the greater the impact you'll experience.

1. **Adopt an abundant mentality:** Be open to believing that opportunities and high-ticket clients are abundant and available to you.

2. **Practice Resilience:** Start viewing challenges as opportunities for growth, not as setbacks. Even when it feels tough, train yourself to find the wins in every situation. This mindset is crucial, especially when dealing with what some may call 'failures'. I intentionally avoid using the word failure by itself — I simply don't believe in it. To me, failure can't exist without the accompanying opportunity to improve ourselves and our services and become better. In business, especially in high-ticket sales, we must see setbacks as stepping stones toward growth, improvement and, ultimately, success. You'll often hear

me say, *"Look for the win in every situation because there's always one."* I invite you to do the same; you'll thank me for it later. We'll explore how to apply this in-depth, both for yourself and your clients, in the **'Proven Results'** chapter later in the book.

3. **Set clear, SMART, financial goals:** Align your actions with these specific goals to attract the high-ticket clients you desire. Clear, measurable goals give you the focus and direction needed to take aligned actions that lead to success, especially in attracting high-ticket clients.

4. **Practice daily gratitude:** Gratitude is the quickest way to shift from a 'low vibe' to feeling empowered and at the top of your game. Think about it, whenever you pause to appreciate the people and things in your life, you instantly feel better and you often attract more of what you're grateful for. Gratitude works in every area because it elevates your energy and invites more abundance. I encourage you to practice it daily — when you wake up and before you sleep as a minimum, and throughout the day once it's become a habit. It's the fastest way to amplify your sense of abundance and it will make attracting and converting high-paying clients feel more effortless.

5. **Visualise your goals daily:** Your subconscious thrives on specificity and repetition. Just like with your money mantras and affirmations, the more vivid and detailed your visualisations are, the more likely they will manifest — provided you take the aligned action (as outlined in step three). One of the key differences between those who achieve success and those who don't is the power of specific visualisation. Take Olympic athletes, for example. They don't just rely on strategy to win gold. They repeatedly visualise crossing the finish line first, feeling the triumph, imagining what they'll wear and experiencing the exact emotions of victory. The same principle applies to visualising your business

and life goals. When it comes to the money you want to make and the high-ticket clients you want to attract, be crystal clear. Visualise the exact amounts you want to generate and the ideal clients you want to work with and imagine these things in the present tense. Picture yourself showing up confidently, charging your worth and converting the calibre of clients you dream of working with. Go deep into how these results make you feel and how life is different for you, your family and those around you now that you're achieving your revenue goals. The more specific, consistent and emotionally charged your visualisations are, the more powerful they'll be in turning your goals into reality.

6. **Reframe any limiting beliefs:** To cultivate a wealth mindset, it's essential to consistently rewire any negative thoughts or beliefs you hold around money and attracting high-ticket clients. Shift these limiting beliefs into empowering ones that support your success and allow you to confidently attract the clients and income you desire. By actively challenging and reframing these thoughts, you'll create a mindset that aligns with the abundance and opportunities you're aiming for.

By cultivating your wealth mindset and implementing these six key principles, you'll not only be equipped to attract high-ticket clients but also create a business that generates the lasting success you want.

BUILDING YOUR HIGH-TICKET IDENTITY

Your ideal high-ticket clients are seeking inspiration, courage and a leader they can trust — someone who embodies their vision and mission. If you're not demonstrating that level of leadership and courage to lead and drive, ask yourself: *"Why should they invest in me?"*

I know those mindset monkeys might be creeping in trying to stop you from becoming the go-to expert for high-ticket clients and from getting paid the high revenue months you want, so let me be honest with you — there are high-ticket clients in your niche and in your audience right now, ready to invest in services like yours. Anyone you see consistently converting high-ticket clients and hitting the high-revenue months you aspire to didn't start there. They began from a similar place to where you may be right now. They began at the beginning. They, too, had to make the decision to go for it, just like you're doing now. You're not alone, so I want you to remember to trust the process I'm guiding you through because it works.

Owning your high-ticket identity means becoming the strategic, mindset and energetic match for premium clients — those who will invest in you in exchange for your expert services. This requires a significant energetic shift. It's not just about what you do; it's more about who you become… your identity. To create an immediate shift, I invite you to think about experts you know of who charge premium prices, deliver outstanding client results and inspire you. How do they show up strategically, energetically and in their mindset? Write down your reflections to create a quick action plan that bridges the gap between where you are now and the level you need to reach to consistently attract high-ticket clients.

Building and embodying your high-ticket identity is about becoming the person, and the leader, who attracts premium clients. It's about how you lead yourself, setting the pace and taking radical responsibility for the high-ticket clients, income and impact you desire. This is the core of the high-ticket game.

YOUR HIGH-TICKET IDENTITY EXERCISE:

To help you along this journey, here are some journal prompts for you to reflect on:

- Are you fully committed to leading from the front, in the belief that you are the go-to expert for high-ticket clients?
- Are you energetically aligned with the identity of someone who attracts high-ticket clients?
- What changes do you need to make to bridge the gap between where you are and where you need to be?
- How do you currently perceive the value of your offers, and what can you do to elevate them?
- What limiting beliefs do you hold around high-ticket clients? Challenge these logically, list them out and then disprove them with facts. Reframe them into empowering beliefs that will serve you moving forward.

It's time for you to step up and take up space as the go-to expert for high-ticket clients in your industry.

To embody your high-ticket identity, there are three core elements you must master:

1. **Confidence and self-worth:** Your high-ticket identity needs to be built on unshakable confidence that you are the expert your ideal, premium-paying clients need and a deep sense of self-worth. High-ticket clients need certainty that you're the expert they're seeking. Your confidence gives them that certainty, so, it's time to claim it — and get ready for those Stripe notifications to start rolling in!

2. **Value perception:** It's your job to be the first to see the premium value in your offers. When you fully believe in the high-value and life-changing transformation of what you're offering, others will too. This applies even to your free content. In the POWER Offer chapter, later in this book, I'll show you how to build that value perception.

3. **Premium positioning:** To consistently attract high-ticket clients, you need to position yourself as the leading authority in your field. I'll dive deeper into this in the 'Perception' chapter, where you'll learn how to become the go-to expert for your ideal high-ticket clients.

Remember, you have the power to step into this high-ticket identity right now. The premium clients and consistent high-revenue months you're aiming for are out there—it's just up to you to go and claim them.

CONFIDENCE-BUILDING STRATEGIES FOR HIGH-TICKET SALES: THE KEY TO CONVERTING PREMIUM CLIENTS

As you've likely realised by now, confidence is the cornerstone of attracting high-ticket clients. It's your secret weapon for positioning yourself as the go-to authority in your industry and securing clients willing to invest at a premium level.

Why is confidence so critical in high-ticket sales? I'll emphasise this throughout the book: premium clients are looking for a confident expert. Your belief in your expertise and your ability to deliver the results they desire is essential. It provides them with the sense of safety and peace of mind they need to make a significant investment. Your confidence is their safety net. While high-ticket sales involve more than just confidence, a lack of it in your expertise, your offers and how you show up will result in a lack of premium clients. Confidence not only shows that you're committed to getting results, but it also builds credibility and trust, and fosters effective communication, all of which are critical for becoming the trusted authority in your industry.

When high-ticket clients feel secure in your expertise, they see investing in you as the fastest way to achieve bigger results, with the peace of mind that they won't be risking their time or money. In turn, they'll be ready and waiting to hire and pay you without hesitation. The good news? Confidence is a skill you can develop, learn and train yourself to embody. So, if you're not feeling fully confident right now, know that this can absolutely change.

For perspective, there are experts out there getting paid £100k+ for their services who are nowhere near as good as you at what it is you do. If they can do it, so can you. The difference lies in their belief in their value and their willingness to confidently charge for it. High-ticket clients exist at every level; it's just about stepping into your high-ticket identity, positioning yourself powerfully and realising that there's no reason why you can't achieve similar results too.

You don't have to be the highest certified or most experienced in your industry to become the best-known or the highest-paid. One of my mentors told me that and it stuck with me. Confidence isn't about being the most qualified; it's about showing up, standing out, and positioning yourself as the go-to expert, who also gets world-class results. By consistently putting yourself out there and taking up space with conviction whilst you co-create incredible life-changing results with your clients, you'll become the trusted authority premium-paying clients are looking for, regardless of how crowded the market may be.

The inner work we've covered in this chapter will empower you to shift your wealth mindset and embody your high-ticket identity. This is the foundation for attracting consistent high-ticket clients, creating elevated impact and driving the income you desire. It all starts with your upgraded sense of self, authority and confidence. Remember, your external success, both financial and physical, will never exceed your internal success. If you know there's room for growth here, now is the time to put in the work.

ACCESS YOUR EXCLUSIVE HIGH-TICKET MASTERY MINI-COURSE

Simply go to **bit.ly/Highticketmethodbookcourse** to unlock your Chapter Two resources giving you further insights into your high-ticket psychology. It's free!

THREE
DECODING YOUR IDEAL HIGH-TICKET CLIENT PSYCHOLOGY

WHAT HIGH-TICKET CLIENTS WANT: THE KEYS TO WINNING THEIR BUSINESS

"IN UNDERSTANDING THE PSYCHOLOGY OF YOUR IDEAL, HIGH-TICKET CLIENT LIES THE KEY TO UNLOCKING A WORLD OF PREMIUM SOLUTIONS: CLIENTS WHO DON'T QUESTION YOUR VALUE, UNWAVERING LOYALTY, IMPACT AND INCOME."

— TANIA KING-MOHAMMAD

What do high-ticket clients really want before they hire you and throw down the big bucks? Let's break it down.

Decoding the psychology of your ideal, high-ticket client isn't just a fun exercise, it's the golden ticket to unlocking a sales process that feels effortless. When you truly understand their needs, desires and aspirations, something transformational happens. Selling high-ticket offers stops feeling like a hard sell and starts feeling like the natural outcome of the powerful solution you're offering. Suddenly, they see you, want you and are more than happy to pay you for your unparalleled and unquestionable value.

To master your niche and be seen as the undeniable go-to expert in your industry that premium-paying clients choose and hire requires you to step up and own your next-level self and your high-ticket identity as the go-to expert for high-ticket clients, with full authenticity and a healthy dose of audacity. This doesn't mean you necessarily have to get 'cocky' about who you are, but it does mean that you need to have full ownership of what you uniquely bring to the table.

For high-ticket clients to hire and pay you quickly, they need to see two things: firstly, that you are the unquestionable expert in your field and secondly, that you have a well-defined niche.

STEP ONE: OWNING YOUR EXPERT STATUS (WITHOUT THE IMPOSTER SYNDROME)

Let's clear something up right now and debunk a potential myth which you may have around really owning your expert status. It's one which I see time and time again from many entrepreneurs: You are an expert. If you're even thinking of offering high-ticket services, you've got the goods to back it up. But why do so many of us, especially women, shy away from owning it? Let's be real, you'd hardly ever see a man downplay his expertise (even when he probably should), so why do so many incredible women entrepreneurs downplay their true expert status? We women, have years of experience in various careers, client success stories and game-changing skills, and yet, here we are, questioning whether we can call ourselves experts. I see it as a responsibility of mine to help change this rhetoric because I know exactly what your true potential is on the other side of this mental block.

Your subconscious mind is wired to keep you playing small and safe within your comfort zone. How it operates hasn't changed since we were living in caves wearing nothing but loin cloths, and needed it to protect us during times of fight or flight when big predators were hanging around. That subconscious programming is still trying to protect you, but it's also holding you back from stepping into your full expert status. It directly impacts how you own your expert status authentically and audaciously. It's time to change this.

So, what makes you the expert? I teach my clients about the four Cs that define your expert status. The four Cs are the secret sauce to becoming the go-to and best-known in your industry and attracting high-ticket clients who value what you bring to the table. Remember that you must see and embody these four Cs in yourself, and your expert status before you expect anyone else to. So, get ready because we're about to dive into them.

THE FOUR CS OF YOUR HIGH-TICKET EXPERT STATUS

1. Clarity

First up: clarity. This is specifically clarity on who you serve, i.e., who your ideal client is. Here, I am specifically referring to clarity on the ideal client that you want to attract and convert. We're talking crystal clear, laser-focused clarity on the exact type of high-ticket client you want to work with. This isn't the time to play small. If you find yourself staying comfortable by speaking to clients who don't challenge or push you to your next level, that's your mind playing it safe. It's time to get honest:

who do you really want to work with? Who's ready to move fast, pay fast, get results and doesn't need hours of convincing?

Many reasons may be stopping you from speaking directly to the higher calibre clients you really want to work with. It's likely that one reason is that you minimise and dilute your expertise and the result you could create with higher calibre clients because of your current results in your business, because you don't feel *"ready"* for that next-level client, but here's the truth: your value is bigger than your current results. You're here because you're driven by impact, not just income, so, stop speaking to the safe clients and start talking to the higher calibre ones you want because, believe me, this is the fastest way to grow your impact and multiply your income.

2. Conviction

You need to have rock-solid, unwavering conviction in your offers and the value and transformation they create. Believe me, without this unwavering conviction in your offers, you will struggle to sell because nobody else will believe in them before you do. When you switch from seeing sales as awkward, sleazy or pushy and start seeing them as an act of service to your audience and your clients, sales become easy, consistent and effortless

Remember this business 101 fundamental: as entrepreneurs, we are here to solve our ideal client's problems. Give your ideal, high-ticket clients the solution to their problems and you are selling with service, which not only means that you are helping change their life or business, but you're also getting paid for it. It's a win-win situation. So, step into full conviction with your offers and the transformation they provide and you'll see how much easier they sell.

It's time to step away from the mindset that selling is you pushing; you're not pushing, you're providing a solution to a very real problem which your client is facing. And when you're solving a big problem, the perceived value skyrockets. That's when clients happily pay premium prices.

> "THE BIGGER THE PROBLEM YOU SOLVE, THE HIGHER THE PERCEIVED VALUE OF YOUR SOLUTION, THE MORE YOU GET PAID."
>
> — TANIA KING-MOHAMMAD

3. Confidence

High-ticket clients want a confident expert. They need to know that you're not only an expert, but that **you know you're an expert**. It goes without saying that this key principle requires you to have mastered your zone of genius and craft. If you've been following along in this book, we've already worked on building that confidence muscle. This is what will get you seen, hired and paid as the go-to expert for high-ticket clients in your niche. Showing up as the confident expert breeds authority and elevates your expert positioning, which makes it even easier for your ideal, high-ticket clients to buy from you because they've already built the trust and certainty they need. It also speeds up the buying process. I'll show you how to master this in the next chapter.

4. Consistency

Finally, let's talk about consistency. Here, I'm specifically referring to consistency across everything that you do, particularly in your messaging, who you are speaking to in your content and how you help your clients. One thing that will kill your high-ticket client attraction is constantly switching your niche or target audience. This becomes confusing not only for you, but also for your potential ideal clients, and confused people don't buy. They're not going to stick around to figure out what you're doing — they'll move on to someone clear and consistent.

STEP TWO: THE NICHE ADVANTAGE - WHY SPECIFICITY SELLS

You've probably heard the famous Pat Flynn saying, *"The riches are in the niches"*. When you commit to owning a specific niche in your market, you instantly create what I like to call the *"niche advantage"*. You become known for solving one specific problem for one specific group of clients. The time when your name starts getting mentioned in groups, events and so on as the expert in your area, is the golden sign for when you've mastered your niche.

It can be tempting to switch niches when you feel bored of the one you've chosen, or when you're not quite getting the results you want. You may also be beyond this stage in business, where you're already known as the expert in your niche. But if you're not, my simple advice is to keep going and to stay consistent with your niche, because if you don't, as I've already said, you'll confuse your audience which means they definitely won't buy.

If you're struggling to niche down, it might be because you're tempted to speak to everyone, fearing that narrowing your focus to just one ideal client will limit your opportunities. But by trying to appeal to everyone, you risk confusing your ideal clients and pushing them toward experts who are clear and consistent in their messaging. We don't want that. We want them to stick around in your world.

> "WHEN YOU SPEAK TO EVERYONE, YOU SPEAK TO NO ONE."
>
> — MEREDITH HILL

Think of Harrods, the luxury London store known for attracting premium clients who are ready to spend on high-ticket items. Now, imagine if Harrods started using marketing tactics like *"Buy two, get one free"* or *"Bargain sale now on"*, similar to the offers you'd see in a high-street shop like Spa or the Co-op. Their premium buyers would likely become very confused and turned off. They would switch from shopping at Harrods to shopping elsewhere at other exclusive stores that maintain their luxury appeal through their message and marketing. Harrods isn't afraid to niche down and speak only and directly to their ideal premium client, nor are they worried about alienating those who aren't a fit. They've mastered high-ticket sales and psychology by staying true to their niche. If you want more consistent high-ticket clients, think like Harrods.

So, what exactly is the niche advantage? It allows you to speak directly to, attract and convert a specific ideal client with a specific problem. This clarity helps you build your reputation and credibility faster because you become known for solving a particular problem. As a result, your business grows faster.

I'm going to give you an example which I love to use when teaching my clients the niche advantage. Imagine that you're getting a new kitchen installed in your home. It's something that you can't wait to get done because you know that your kitchen is the heart of your home, and you can't wait to show it off by hosting dinner parties for your family and friends. It's something important to you. It's also something that you're willing to invest thousands in, with the right expert to do it for you because you know that your existing kitchen just doesn't cut it anymore for your living and entertaining purposes. So, it comes to choosing the builder, the expert you'll hire to get the job done. You've got two choices: Bob, the general builder who's done a few kitchens in his time but who also does bathrooms, loft conversions and decking, or Chris the kitchen fitter, the guy who only does kitchens, day in and day out. You'd choose Chris every time, right? Because you perceive Chris as the expert because kitchens are all he does.

By hiring Chris, you'd also likely expect fewer problems and therefore less risk, because he's the go-to kitchen fitter and the expert in this field. You'll probably also be prepared to wait a bit longer for Chris to do the work, and you'd probably be prepared to pay him more than if Bob was to say he could do it now. Your choice of hiring Chris all comes down to the niche advantage. He's known as the expert in his field for his specific thing. He solves one specific problem, kitchens. He therefore has higher perceived value when it comes to kitchens than Bob and, as a result, can charge more. Chris' name will also be mentioned more in his community when it comes to anyone asking for recommendations on a kitchen fitter. Chris is smart. Chris has the niche advantage. And that's what we're aiming for. Be like Chris.

THE POWER OF NICHING DOWN

If you're struggling to identify what your niche is, here are five essential niche elements to help you decide and stick to the niche of your choice, so you become the go-to expert that premium clients hire.

1. Passion

You must be passionate about your niche. Passion drives success and profitability. It gives you the fuel to push forward, even when business gets challenging. Without it, you'll find it hard to maintain the energy and commitment required to build a thriving business, particularly when times get tough.

2. Expertise

You need to be the expert in your niche. You need to have mastered your zone of genius. The good news here is that if you're new to your niche or business, don't worry, many of the skills you've developed in previous roles will be transferable to your new business. It's important not to discount these just because you've started something new. If you're struggling to own your expertise, I have a simple but powerful exercise which I ask my clients to do when they have a similar challenge: write down twenty or more reasons why you're the go-to expert in your field and why high-ticket clients should hire you. It might feel awkward or hard at first, but it's an empowering exercise that will help you recognise the value you bring to the table. I want you to get at least twenty down – more, if you can. My guess is once you get going with this, you will actually enjoy it.

3. Viability

Do your research and make sure that there is demand for your niche. A great way to confirm this is to look for successful competitors in the space. As a warning, this might trigger some self-doubt (enter the mindset monkeys again — *"They're already doing it and are already successful, so there's no way I can, why should I bother?"*), but that's a sign your potential niche is viable and very likely profitable. There's always room for more. Think of all the estate agents across the UK. There are multiple on the same street in any town across the UK, yet they all thrive, otherwise they wouldn't be there. Did the fact that there were already lots of agencies on the same street stop them from setting up shop? No. So don't let potential competition in your niche stop you. There is room and there are clients for everyone. Your niche can accommodate you too.

4. Demand for Premium Offers

To sell high-ticket and premium offers successfully, there has to be demand for them within your niche. A great way to test this is to run a focus group with your ideal high-ticket clients to gauge what the interest is in your proposed high-ticket offers or services. This will give you valuable insight into what they are looking for and if they're willing to pay for premium solutions.

5. Financial Accessibility

Your ideal clients need to have the financial means to invest in your premium services. There's no point in creating and launching a premium offer to an audience who simply can't afford it, so save yourself the time and effort and do your background checks on this first. It's vital to ensure that you're positioning yourself in a niche where there are clients who can afford to pay high-ticket prices.

Now, in some instances, your niche may go beyond purely just the subject matter. Points for you to consider here are the characteristics and energetics of your ideal clients. In these cases, your focus would be more on who your clients are as people rather than the specific topic you help with.

EXERCISE:
KEY QUESTIONS TO ASK YOURSELF TO HELP SUPPORT YOU WHEN DEFINING YOUR NICHE:

- What is your unique expertise?
- What are your hobbies and interests?
- What are you passionate about?
- Do your ideal clients have the financial means to invest?
- Is there a demand for premium offers in this niche?
- Is there a problem in this niche that you can solve and that premium clients will pay high-ticket prices for?

My advice for you is once you've decided on your niche, stick to it. Don't change it until your name is being thrown around as the go-to expert in your space. This will feel challenging at times, especially when it seems like no one is watching or buying, but trust me, if you stay consistent, it will pay off. Keep going. It's worth it, I promise.

PERSONALISED EXPERIENCES MATTER

Have you ever paid more for something because it made you feel you were paying for something exclusive? Or that the service made you feel like a VIP? This is exactly what high-ticket clients are looking for and are prepared to pay for, in addition to hiring you because you are the confident expert they're looking for. High-ticket clients are willing to pay more for this kind of exclusivity. It's not just about being good at what you do; it's about making your clients feel like they're getting something bespoke and tailor-made, just for them.

Personalised experiences are the key to creating a sense of exclusivity. This means that when someone invests in an offer, service or product tailored just for them, they feel that they're investing in something that feels special and not available to the masses. High-ticket clients face unique challenges or 'problems' that they'll hire you to solve. But they're looking for a bespoke, personalised solution, not a 'one size fits all' cookie-cutter approach. This elevated sense of perceived value means premium buyers are willing to invest more in personalised experiences.

We'll dive deeper into the psychology of personalised experiences later in the book, but it's important to mention this here: if you want to charge premium prices, make your clients feel like they're getting a premium experience.

LEVERAGING YOUR NICHE ADVANTAGE

In summary, when it comes to getting the niche advantage, decide on your niche, commit to it and show up as the expert in your niche consistently. Don't jump from one niche to another every time things feel challenging, or you feel you're not quite getting your desired results. Stick with it until you're the name on everyone's lips when they need a go-to expert to provide a solution in your area of expertise.

Stay consistent, stay confident, and remember: the high-ticket clients you want are out there waiting for you to step up and own your expertise. And when you do, they'll see you, hire you and pay you, without question.

THE FOUR EXPERT VALUES

In this section, we'll explore how personalised experiences, combined with your confidence as the expert, create the **Four Expert Values** that high-ticket clients seek:

- Bigger Results and ROI
- Speed

- Convenience
- Reduced Risk

The four expert values are what high-ticket clients will hire and pay you for as their chosen go-to expert. I want to showcase exactly what each of these means and how you can communicate each of them in your marketing to drive more high-ticket sales ethically within your business. Later in this book, we'll delve deeper into promoting and delivering your sought-after personalised experiences in a chapter dedicated entirely to this.

Bigger Results and ROI. Premium-paying clients recognise that your services and offers create significant transformations. This requires you to go above and beyond the ordinary in terms of how you show up and market yourself, your authority, positioning and the value and results your offers deliver. To express the results your offers create requires you to consistently showcase your client results and testimonials in your marketing to provide social proof, highlighting the specific outcomes both you and your clients have achieved and what new clients can expect when they invest in your services.

Speed. Time is everyone's most valuable asset, especially for high-ticket clients who prioritise efficiency. Your job is to demonstrate that by working with you, clients can expect quicker results and that by implementing your unique methodology, your clients are able to speed up their progress. Highlight how your process accelerates their journey by sharing your results, emphasising the time-saving benefits and faster progress they can expect by investing in you and your offers or services.

Convenience. A seamless, convenient experience will appeal to premium buyers, especially one which makes achieving their goals feel easier and more accessible. This can involve delivering tailored bespoke services, flexible processes and personalised attention to ensure their journey with you is hassle-free and enjoyable, compared to if they were to go it alone. In your marketing, showcase how your unique methodology streamlines the process for your clients and highlight all the resources they have access to, proving that you provide a complete turnkey experience where everything they need to achieve their goals is included for them.

Reduced Risk. Premium buyers need assurance from you that their investment is low risk. By confidently positioning yourself as the expert in your niche, by showcasing your unwavering conviction that you are the confident expert and by highlighting that your services are designed and proven to create faster results with more ease than if clients were to try achieving their goals alone, you build trust and mitigate any perceived risks in their decision to hire you.

How you showcase the reduced risk associated with your offers will look like consistently sharing your client successes to illustrate that your unique methodology works. You may also consider offering money-back guarantees or trial periods to further reassure potential clients.

Communicate these four expert values across your marketing efforts and you'll multiply your impact and income faster than before by establishing yourself as the in-demand expert for high-ticket clients.

IDENTIFYING YOUR HIGH-TICKET CLIENT PERSONA

When thinking about clarifying your ideal, high-ticket client, I'd like you to start thinking about the following points:

- Who would you be most excited to work with? Picture them walking into your office and saying, *"I want to work with you; money is no issue. When can we start?"*. You need to feel energised by the prospect of working with this person.

- Avoid thinking, *"I should/could work with this type of client"*. Instead, ask yourself, *"Who do I genuinely want to work with if there are no limits on the clients I could attract and serve?"*.

- Choose an ideal, high-ticket client who lights you up! Business should be exciting. By attracting clients who inspire you, your business and work will feel lighter, fun and more enjoyable. After all, if business isn't fun most of the time, you're probably not doing it right.

This is your opportunity to think big and give yourself permission to attract the clients you dream of working with, rather than settling for the clients you think you could manage. By doing this, I guarantee that once you start attracting the higher calibre, premium clients you really want to work with, business will feel lighter, exciting and fun, because you're working with clients who don't need convincing or persuading to work with you or who consistently tell you that your prices are too high (let's face it, there's nothing that makes you feel more undervalued than this), and you're working with the type of clients who are committed to doing the work to get the elevated results and ROI which you co-create together.

☆❗

CLIENT TRANSFORMATION

Let's talk about Kate, a client who came to work with me to elevate her business and achieve industry-leading success. Although she was already doing well, consistently attracting clients who paid up to £3,000, her goal was to draw in clients willing to invest closer to £10,000 each week.

Kate's aspirations were nothing short of audacious, even though she wasn't sure how to get there. Coming from a humble background, the thought of earning high-income months was intimidating. She doubted whether it was even possible for her, but deep down, she knew she wanted to try. To achieve these goals, she understood she needed the right support to establish herself as a leader in her niche and attract high-ticket clients.

At the time, Kate was doing well, but aimed for consistent higher multi-five-figure months. The reason she wanted to reach this goal was that it would allow her to retire her husband, spend quality time with her children and not have to feel like she had to be stuck to her phone 24/7, which is what business felt like up to this point.

Despite her skill set, Kate struggled to embrace her position as a leader in her industry. Her fear of being judged kept her voice small and led her to dilute her message. She held back from creating the impactful content she really wanted to produce and the elevated positioning she knew she needed.

Together, we worked on overcoming these barriers using my high-ticket frameworks. We refined her offer suite to make it irresistible and developed a clear and profitable product suite that aligned with her newly elevated authority and messaging.

Initially, Kate felt uncomfortable and terrified by my authority-building high-ticket frameworks we were implementing. However, she leaned into the support I provided and committed to implementing our work.

In just three months of our collaboration, Kate's monthly revenue skyrocketed from doing well in her business to her first consistent cash months just shy of £50,000 each.

Kate came to work with me with big dreams of achieving consistent high-income months, yet she lacked a roadmap to get there. By recognising the value of getting the right support and going all-in on her goals, she has set herself on a path to incredible success. I predict that within the next twelve months, Kate will be hitting the six-figure monthly income she desires.

To conclude chapter three, without mastering your ideal, high-ticket client persona, any attempts to enhance your business — like hiring a social media manager, implementing funnels, running paid ads or selling your offers — simply won't work. Trust me, I've been there and it's not fun! Don't skip this important step; you'll thank me later, I promise.

ACCESS YOUR EXCLUSIVE HIGH-TICKET MASTERY MINI-COURSE

Simply go to **bit.ly/Highticketmethodbookcourse** to access your Chapter Three resources and dive deeper into the psychology of your ideal high-ticket client.

FOUR
THE ANATOMY OF A PREMIUM BRAND

How your audience perceives you shapes their reality of how they measure your value and ultimately, how much they are willing to pay to work with you. In this chapter, we define what makes a premium brand, so you can start bringing this into your brand and business to start attracting the higher-level, premium-paying clients you want to work with.

> "YOUR BRAND IS WHAT OTHER PEOPLE SAY ABOUT YOU WHEN YOU'RE NOT IN THE ROOM."
>
> — JEFF BEZOS

It's important to clarify that when I refer to 'brand', I'm not talking about attractive colours or a pretty logo. Sure, there is absolutely a place for these in your brand, which we'll cover shortly, but instead, I'm referring to the *essence* that underlines a powerful and premium brand. I'm referring to the emotions and experiences which your audience and clients have when they interact with you and your brand. So, in this chapter, I will encourage you to reflect on how you want your audience and clients to feel when they interact and work with you and your brand, helping you embody those feelings from the outset, to ultimately drive more conversions, sales and impact.

> "A BRAND GOES FAR BEYOND INFORMATION; IT'S A FEELING, AN EXPERIENCE. CREATE THE RESULTS, EXPERIENCES AND FEELINGS YOUR IDEAL CLIENTS DESIRE, AND YOU'LL NEVER STRUGGLE TO MAKE SALES AGAIN."
>
> — TANIA KING-MOHAMMAD

In today's competitive entrepreneurial market, where the online space is increasingly saturated with noise and distraction, establishing a premium brand is not just a luxury, it's essential. A strong premium brand will distinguish you from the crowd, allowing you to be seen and heard amidst the chaos of those who are simply just adding to the noise.

Imagine this – sales are coming into your business consistently, every offer that you promote sells immediately, you're filling your high-ticket offers quickly and with ease and you're making the consistent higher monthly revenue you've always wanted. This is what a powerful premium brand will do for you, with sales practically waltzing right in without the need to persuade or convince clients to buy. *"What a relief!"* I hear you say! It builds your reputation as the in-demand expert, promotes trust in what you do and makes your offers irresistible and compelling for your ideal high-ticket clients who can't resist them.

My first piece of advice when it comes to you building your high-ticket brand, is to start treating your brand, offers and sales like you know people want it and will buy everything you launch.

ELEVATE YOUR BRAND, MULTIPLY YOUR IMPACT AND SALES

To succeed in ethical high-ticket sales, your brand is your most valuable asset. It's not just about what you offer; it's about the perception, energy, value and authority you project and evoke in your audience and clients. As an example, if you position yourself as the best in your field but offer the lowest prices, you risk diminishing your perceived value and authority in the eyes of your audience due to a mismatch between what you're saying you are, versus your brand perception and pricing.

Instead, focus on building a powerful high-ticket brand that reflects the true value of the transformations you provide. By elevating your prices to match the world-class value you deliver, you'll see your brand's perceived value skyrocket, along with your sales. Remember, it's not just about what you sell; it's about the experience and results your clients receive when they choose to interact and work with you.

There are three key elements that make up a high-ticket brand:

1. **Elevated Value Perception and Authority:** Your brand directly influences how your audience perceives your value in the market, and in-turn, how much clients will be prepared to pay you. It's the direct bridge between how your services are perceived by your audience and your ideal clients investing in your services.

2. **Positive Influence on Sales:** There is a direct connection between a powerful high-ticket brand and increased

sales. The stronger your brand, the more likely you are to see your sales skyrocket.

3. **Elevated Market Position:** A strong brand is the vehicle for you to charge higher prices. It enhances your positioning as a leader in the market and builds greater trust among your clients.

A strong brand not only allows you to charge higher prices, but also helps you to justify those prices by elevating the trust your audience has in you and your brand. This is achieved in six key ways:

- **Elevated Value Perception**: This reflects how your audience views you. By enhancing the perceived value beyond your actual offers, you help justify higher price points in the minds of your audience.

- **Trust and Reliability**: A strong brand increases the willingness and trust of your audience to invest in your services at higher price points.

- **Emotional Connection**: By creating a powerful high-ticket brand that resonates with your ideal high-ticket clients, you can build deeper connections with your audience and future clients. This emotional bond encourages their willingness to invest at higher price points.

- **Market Differentiation**: Standing out in a crowded online space is crucial. A strong high-ticket brand enhances the perceived value your audience has of you, leading them to psychologically justify your premium pricing which is in alignment with how they perceive your elevated brand.

- **Perceived Value vs. Cost**: A compelling premium brand shifts any focus that your potential clients may have about your offers and prices from cost to value. This shift enables and psychologically justifies investing in your premium pricing in the minds of your ideal clients — this is exactly what you want as the expert catering to high-ticket clients in your industry.

- **Long-Term Relationships:** Through building strong connections and resonance with your ideal, high-ticket buyers, you not only secure long-term clients but also cultivate long-term loyal advocates for your brand. When clients love what you do and what you stand for, they become passionate and loyal supporters of your business.

WHAT IS A PERSONAL BRAND?

A personal brand is how you make those in your audience and clients feel when they interact with you, as the face of your brand. It's the emotions you evoke in them when they think of your brand and what you stand for. Literally speaking, your personal brand is made up of your unique combination of skills, experiences, personality and values which you want your brand to be known for. It encompasses how you market yourself, your expertise and exactly what sets you apart from the rest of your industry (this last point is key).

It's important to get your personal brand right because it reflects your reputation, both professionally and personally.

The easiest way to create a powerful personal brand is to simply be your authentic self – after all, it's your uniqueness that ultimately determines why clients choose to buy from you amongst all the others in your niche… or not.

ESTABLISHING YOURSELF AS THE UNRIVALED AUTHORITY IN YOUR INDUSTRY

Authority in the high-ticket space isn't just about selling; it's about establishing yourself with a reputation as the go-to expert in your niche for the problem you solve. Becoming a non-negotiable authority influences how you are perceived by your ideal high-ticket clients. You establish yourself as the go-to authority through thought leadership and sharing your thoughts and opinions on key topics that you feel strongly about which, by the way, may sometimes feel slightly uncomfortable. It involves being unafraid of showcasing your expertise, consistent visibility and embodiment of the four Cs covered in the previous chapter: clarity on who you serve, conviction in your offers and services, confidence in your expertise and consistency across all that you do.

CRAFTING YOUR PREMIUM BRAND IDENTITY

By crafting a clear high-ticket brand identity, you build the strong foundation you need for attracting and retaining the high-ticket clients you want to work with (we'll delve deeper into achieving high client retention levels in Chapter Nine of this book). Your high-ticket brand identity acts as a magnet for these clients. It shapes their perception of your value and authority, as well as that of your brand and offers.

Key elements specific to high-ticket brands that you need to be aware of include detachment from the outcome of any potential sales, building high levels of trust and confidence and delivering an elevated client experience. This is achieved by always asking yourself, *"How can I consistently elevate my client experience and client satisfaction levels?"*. Finally, you need to adopt a long-term mindset for a sustainable business built on solid foundations.

At this stage, when working with my clients on elevating their premium brands, I take them through my Seven-step Premium Brand Framework, shown below.

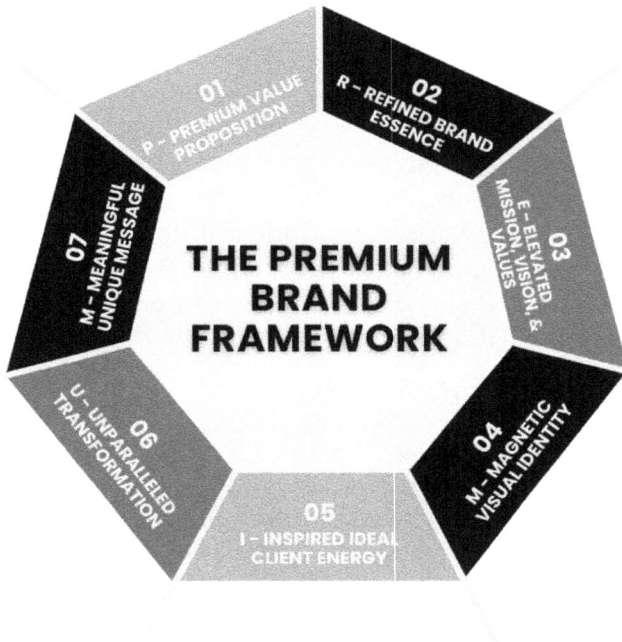

This framework provides the essential seven elements you need to build your premium brand with ease. To make it even easier for you to remember, and because I love simplicity, the first letters of each step in this framework spell out *"Premium."* Now, let's dive in and start creating your premium brand!

THE PREMIUM BRAND FRAMEWORK

PILLAR ONE: PREMIUM AND UNIQUE VALUE PROPOSITION

In a crowded entrepreneurial space, authenticity is key. We don't need more inauthentic copies of someone else in the entrepreneurial space. What we do need more of, is experts owning their unique genius, audaciously. People buy from an expert because of their unique approach, not because they're a fake, watered-down version of someone else. Even though there may be hundreds or thousands of others doing exactly what you do in your niche, when it comes to your ideal client's buying decision, they'll choose the right expert for them based on their uniqueness. This is your reminder that your ideal, premium-paying clients will choose you based on what sets you apart. Nobody has the same experience as you or teaches what you do, in the way you do. This is your superpower, so now is the time to own it!

Don't fall into the trap of copying what others are doing. Remember, as entrepreneurs, the highest paid of us will be the ones who do things differently. Be bold. Showcase what makes you different and what makes you, you! It's the key thing that will get you the clients you want and as a by-product, make you the most money.

Defining your unique value proposition means defining your unique story and distinctiveness, your brand is a story that never stops being told. It's always evolving. It's the evolution of your journey, your achievements, your expertise, your challenges and your purpose. We'll dive into these in **Pillar Four** of the Premium Brand Framework.

To craft your premium and unique value proposition, I encourage you to focus on three elements:

First, identify your unique story. Your story is what makes you unique. This means identifying the key milestones in your journey – where you started, why you decided to make a change, the results and impact you've achieved since and exactly how you did it. Nobody else in your industry has your unique story and this is what will make you stand out.

Second, clarify your unique methodology. For example, throughout this book, I take you step-by-step through my six-step system, *The High-Ticket Method*®. Having your own unique system or methodology instantly positions you as the authority in your niche and fosters professionalism and credibility. In basic terms, it means you know your sh*t.

Third, outline exactly why your clients should choose you over others. This should include your qualifications, accolades, expertise, results, client results and what makes you different to everyone else. Don't worry if you don't have qualifications or accolades, but if you do, use them.

This process allows you to highlight your uniqueness, which you'll then bring into your marketing, content and future speaking engagements to differentiate you from everyone else in your niche. To do this, it's also important to communicate your unparalleled brand value, so think about how you can showcase your difference in brand identity and value, a unique combination which only you bring to the table. Powerful ways to do this include positioning yourself as a thought leader by expressing your opinions of common topics in your niche and general topics in the world and showcasing the benefits of working with your brand above any competition.

When focusing on building a premium brand, it's important to outline how your brand and unique premium value proposition create an exclusive experience tailored to your high-paying clients. It's your job to make working with you and investing in your services a 'must-have' because you're too good to be labelled a 'nice-to-have'.

Here, I want to give you an example of my brand's unique value proposition, which may help get your creative juices flowing to create yours:

Tania's Unique Value Proposition:

- Dr Tania King-Mohammad, The Wealth Strategist.
- Mother, wife, daughter, doctor and high-ticket sales strategist for powerhouse CEOs
- I don't just help you multiply your income online with high-ticket clients; I advocate for 360° wealth-building and have built a seven-figure property portfolio.
- I am a serial entrepreneur, not just a 'one-trick pony'.
- My brand represents building an extraordinary, freedom-fueled lifestyle by design and a legacy.
- I represent the possibility of building successful businesses as a mother to young children. All my businesses were started after my first daughter was born. If I can, you can.

EXERCISE: DEFINING YOUR PREMIUM AND UNIQUE VALUE PROPOSITION

Now it's your turn to define, create or re-create your own unique value proposition. Follow these simple steps to define what sets you apart:

Step One: Define Your Story

- Identify key moments in your journey that led you to where you are today.
- What transformation have you achieved, and why did you choose this path?

Step Two: Clarify Your Methodology

- What unique method, process or approach do you take your clients through to help them achieve results? If you're just starting out it's okay, I don't want you to get overwhelmed, just think of the steps you've taken yourself to get you where you are today and turn this into a logical step-by-step method or process.
- Name your method or system to make it stand out.

Step Three: Highlight Your Expertise

- Why should clients choose you? Focus on results, expertise and what makes you different.

Step Four: Craft Your Value Proposition

- Combine your story, methodology and expertise into a short, powerful statement about what you offer and why clients should choose you.

By completing this exercise, you'll have a clear, compelling statement for your brand that sets you apart as a premium brand.

PILLAR TWO: REFINED BRAND ESSENCE

Your brand goes far beyond just delivering information. If that were all that mattered, people would just use Google to solve their problems rather than invest in an expert to help them. Instead, your brand represents the feelings and emotions you evoke in your audience and clients when they interact and engage with you.

Pinpointing these emotions is essential to building a brand that resonates with your ideal client.

To take it up a step further and elevate your brand into the premium arena, focus on creating a sense of sophistication and exclusivity. You do this by limiting the availability of your offers to drive down supply and create demand. Make sure your pricing equates to the higher perceived value you need your ideal, high-ticket buyers to associate with your brand.

Every interaction that your audience and clients have with your brand should reinforce the essence, energy and refined brand identity you want to portray with consistency. Consistency with this across your brand's aesthetics, messaging, lifestyle and leadership is what creates a lasting impression. It's this consistency that creates and builds trust and speeds up the buying process with your potential clients.

Below is an example of my refined brand essence to help you create yours:

My Brand - Dr Tania King-Mohammad, The Wealth Strategist
Brand essence:

- Wealthy but approachable
- Wealthy but self-made
- Aspirational yet relatable
- Confident and impactful
- Brave, honest and caring
- An ethical leader with impact, kindness and authority

EXERCISE:
REFINING YOUR BRAND ESSENCE

To help you ensure your brand creates resonance with your ideal high-ticket clients, I've included some powerful key questions for you to use as prompts to help refine your brand essence:

1. What Emotions Do You Want to Evoke?

Write down the top three emotions you want your audience to feel when they interact with your brand (e.g., trust, excitement, empowerment, confidence, luxury, exclusivity).

2. Evaluate Your Brand Alignment

Is your current brand messaging, visuals, and overall presence aligned with evoking these emotions?

- If yes: Identify what's working well.
- If no: What specific changes can you make to bring your brand into alignment? This could involve tweaking your messaging, visuals or how you engage with your audience.

By answering these, you'll be clearer on how you can strengthen your brand's emotional connection with your clients.

PILLAR THREE: ELEVATED VISION, MISSION AND VALUES

If you want to build a brand that attracts your ideal clients, there are three core elements you need in place as your foundation. These are your mission, vision and values.

The first of these to identify is your mission. Your mission is the purpose and objectives of your business — what your business is here to achieve and exactly how it will achieve it. A solid mission is one that goes beyond just profitability. As a premium brand, your mission should embody a purpose which resonates with your brand, clients, audience and the long-term sustainability of your business.

The second is to identify your compelling vision. This is the bigger picture of your brand and business. It's the end result you want your business to achieve. It's the ultimate impact you want to create. To attract the right clients to your brand, it's your job to communicate your brand's vision in a compelling way which resonates with your ideal, high-ticket buyers, one they can connect and identify with. A well-communicated mission and vision can establish your brand as a leader in your industry.

The third is to establish your company values. These are your brand's guiding values which act as the moral compass of your company. They should shape the internal culture of your business and all decisions and interactions should be made in alignment with these values and the overall brand identity. A cohesive internal culture, built on strong guiding values, ensures consistency in how your brand is represented and interpreted and will steer your business decisions, offers, sales, processes and client interactions.

To help you with this, here's an example of my brand's elevated mission, vision and values:

My Brand: Dr. Tania king-Mohammad, The Wealth Strategist

Mission: To empower online entrepreneurs to scale their six-, multi-six- and seven-figure empires by elevating their high-ticket services to create ultimate wealth, impact and freedom. We help you get paid more for the work you love, without multiplying your workload.

Vision: We help entrepreneurs to create real 360° wealth.

Values: Honesty, integrity, freedom, kindness, excellence, transparency, ambition, success and wealth.

EXERCISE:
CRAFTING YOUR ELEVATED VISION, MISSION, AND VALUES

It's time to define the core elements of your business — the foundation on which it is built. I've included the prompts below to help you identify your elevated vision, mission and values to form the solid foundation your business needs for sustainability:

1. What is Your Mission?

Write a clear statement that captures the purpose of your business.

2. What is Your Vision?

Describe the future you aspire to create through your business.

3. Define Your Company Values:

List your core values. Reflect on whether these values align with those of your ideal, high-ticket clients.

4. Create Your Mission Statement:

Craft a concise mission statement that includes:

- Who you are
- Who you help
- How you help them
- The result you help them achieve

By completing this simple but important exercise, you'll build a strong foundation for your brand that will resonate with your audience and help guide your business decisions.

PILLAR FOUR: MAGNETIC VISUAL IDENTITY

When we talk about your brand identity, it's not just about the pretty visuals, aesthetics and logos, although these elements play an important role. To build a trustworthy, premium brand, you need to create a magnetic visual identity that reflects a cohesive, striking and consistent representation of your brand across all platforms.

A visually striking and recognisable brand identity serves as the 'face of your brand' and is often the first impression that your audience and clients get when they first interact with you and your brand.

It needs to align with your refined brand essence — the emotions and feelings you want to evoke in your clients and audience. This means maintaining consistency across all design elements, from colours and fonts to graphics, to create a unified and memorable brand image. Doing so builds trust, credibility and confidence in your brand and facilitates a smoother and faster buying process.

For example, my brand's visual identity is cohesive across all platforms, whether you're visiting my website, **taniakingmohammad.com**, or engaging with me on social media. The fonts, colours and graphics are all designed to convey a premium and sophisticated look to align with my high-ticket niche and brand. This level of cohesion is essential in making your brand visually magnetic. Remember, what your audience sees, they believe, so if you're marketing yourself as the best in your niche but your brand's visual representation doesn't reflect this, there will be a mismatch in your audience's perception of your brand, which will reduce their trust in you and will impact your sales.

By bringing a magnetic visual identity into your brand, you create 'marketplace recognition' and recall among your audience, because your brand's visual identity stands out. Consistency across all the brand materials including font, colours, logos etc., reinforces your brand message and therefore creates more trust, credibility and reliability in your audience with you and your brand and, ultimately, what you stand for.

Here are three key strategies for creating consistency and cohesion across your brand's visual elements to build trust and speed up your client buying process:

1. Create clear visual guidelines: These act as your roadmap for your consistent design across everything created in your business.

2. Use templates and design assets: Using these will make life so much easier for you. It speeds up the creation process while ensuring visual consistency across everything your brand produces.

3. Conduct regular brand audits and reviews: Regularly review your brand's visual identity to make sure it aligns with your brand's mission, vision and values, ensuring relevance to your company mission and brand identity and consistency over time.

EXERCISE: ALIGNING YOUR VISUAL IDENTITY WITH YOUR BRAND'S ENERGY

1. Evaluate Your Visual Identity:

Take a moment to assess your current brand visuals (logo, colours, fonts, etc.). Ask yourself:

- Does your visual identity align with the feeling you want your brand to evoke?

2. Resonance Check:

Consider your ideal client. Reflect on these questions:

- Does your visual identity resonate with the energy of your ideal client?
- If not, identify specific elements that need to change.

By completing this exercise, you'll ensure your visual identity authentically represents your brand and attracts your ideal, higher-paying clients.

PILLAR FIVE: INSPIRED, IDEAL CLIENT ENERGY

To attract your ideal, high-ticket clients, your job is to understand exactly who they are, their mindset and their desires. This allows you to create bespoke offers and experiences that align with what they truly want and, more importantly, need. Evoking the right emotions in your clients means that your brand resonates with them on a deeper level, which positively influences your clients' buying process.

Remember during our work on identifying your ideal, high-ticket client persona previously, I specified that niching down can sometimes mean niching down on the character, personality and energy type of your ideal client, rather than just where they are in life or business. This can apply to your brand too.

As an example, my ideal clients are fun, full of energy, exciting, driven and very ambitious. They are usually extroverts but occasionally introverts, who are ready to challenge themselves to get their desired results and they almost always try to see things from a positive point of view, even when it feels challenging.

Attracting your inspired, ideal client means creating deep connections with them. This is about more than just making transactions. It's about building genuine relationships rooted in trust, confidence and a shared energy. You can deepen this connection by bringing storytelling into your marketing.

Storytelling is a powerful strategy to create resonance and help your ideal, high-ticket clients identify in you, your journey, your clients and your brand. Other strategies you can use in your brand to deepen your connection with your ideal clients include personalised communication such as sending voice notes, inviting them to exclusive offers and surprises, gifts and celebrations and, critically, leading customer service with a client-centric focus, which in the high-ticket space, needs to happen from the moment they find you.

Converting more of your ideal, high-ticket clients requires you to focus on longevity in your business by prioritising and sustaining long-term relationships with your clients and your people. This means moving away from focusing on quick wins, quick sales and short-lived dopamine hits and instead, focusing on the long-term game and sustainability, which is what will create the longevity of relationships and a more sustainable business for you. Remind yourself that you are not here *just* for the quick wins and the big one-off payments. Yes, these are great and exciting and deserve to be celebrated, however, by focusing more on long-term relationships, building genuine connections and attracting clients who commit to staying in our world long-term, you get to build security, stability and sustainability in your business and more in-depth support and impact for your clients. To do this effectively, you need to be clear on and understand your ideal clients' energy.

EXERCISE:
IDENTIFYING YOUR IDEAL CLIENT'S ENERGY AND PERSONALITY

1. Define Your Ideal Client Energy and Personality:
Describe the energy type and personality traits of your ideal, high-ticket client. Consider aspects like their aspirations, values and lifestyle.

2. Assess Your Brand Resonance:

Evaluate whether your brand resonates with and attracts this type of client:

- Does your brand reflect the energy and personality of your ideal client?

3. Identify Any Changes to be Made:

If your brand doesn't align, note specific changes you can make to better attract and resonate with your ideal client.

Completing this exercise will help you ensure your brand connects deeply with the energy and personality type of your target high-ticket clients.

PILLAR SIX: UNPARALLELED TRANSFORMATION

This is where it gets really exciting because the unparalleled transformation you help create with your clients, is what sets you apart from your competition. This is what you do business for. But it goes without saying that for you to communicate how incredible your offers are, you have to be the first to believe in them.

"LET EXCELLENCE BE YOUR BRAND. WHEN YOU ARE EXCELLENT, YOU BECOME UNFORGETTABLE."

— OPRAH WINFREY

To convey this to your ideal clients, it's your job to demonstrate your brand impact. It's not really about the steps or the process; it's about the incredible, life-changing results your services help create. Your job is to showcase this transformation consistently and demonstrate the tangible value and results that your services provide.

To help my clients communicate the life-changing transformation their brands and offers create, one of my favourite analogies is to always remember to sell the beach body, not the gym sessions. Think about it for a moment; if you want to look your best for your upcoming summer holiday – one that you've spent months planning and thousands paying for – when you buy your gym membership to get you there, it's the result you want. You want to feel and look good. You don't 'want' the thirty minutes of cardio five times a week and the weight training that goes with it.

It's not the process that your ideal clients want, it's the tangible end result. This is what clients buy; clients buy the result, not the step-by-step process. As an example, the end tangible result I help my clients create is more money and more freedom to enjoy their lives, so when it comes to selling my offers, I sell these tangible outcomes and transformations. I don't sell the six steps of *The High-Ticket Method*®.

The more clearly and confidently you focus on communicating the unparalleled transformation which your offers create for your clients, the more higher-level clients you will attract and as a result, the more you will get paid. To do this effectively, be clear in your outcome, have conviction in yourself and your services and leave no space for being unsure or uncertain about the transformation you help create. You need to own the transformation you create in order to sell it.

To help with this in your marketing, you need to use conviction-led language and avoid possibility language. As a consumer, I'm sure you've had experiences where the person selling you something wasn't convincing due to the possibility language they used and over-explaining what was included in the offer. Most likely, it ended up with you not purchasing whatever it was they were trying to sell. Had they used language which was more convincing and conviction-led, and had they focused on selling the outcome it would give you, the odds of you buying would have been higher. It's the same when it comes to the sales in your business. Examples of conviction-led language include phrases like, *"By joining us inside this offer, you will multiply your sales and impact,"* and, *"This strategy will 10X your results".* Examples of possibility language include words like *"could", "may"* and *"probably".*

It's important to speak about what your offer statement is at this point. An offer statement is a clear and compelling description of what your offer provides and the value it delivers to your ideal client. It clearly communicates the transformation or results that someone will achieve by purchasing and engaging with your product or service, rather than just outlining the features or the process.

The key components of a strong offer statement are:

1. **End Result** – The tangible transformation or outcome your client will experience.
2. **Ideal Client** – Who the offer is for, ensuring it speaks

directly to them.

3. **Timeframe** (optional, but powerful if you can include this) – If applicable, how long it will take to achieve the result?

4. **Unique Value** – What makes your offer stand out or different from others in the market?

Example of an offer statement:

"By joining my High-Ticket Mastermind, you will get the strategy, tools and support to help you consistently convert premium clients and scale your revenue by 30% within ninety days, without burning out or discounting your offers."

In this example, the end result is scaling revenue by 30% and converting premium clients, the ideal client is entrepreneurs looking to scale and the timeframe is 90 days. It focuses on the transformation, not the steps of how it's done (the process).

An offer statement should quickly convey the value of your offer and why your ideal client should take action.

Another powerful way to showcase the unparalleled transformation which your offers create is to engage your audience through storytelling. Using stories is your opportunity to showcase your expertise and thought leadership and to enable your ideal, premium-paying clients to resonate and identify with your journey and the journey of your existing clients, which is important. This helps them see that the results you are creating are possible for them too, and that these results can also be their reality. What this does is activate them more to take action on your offer, rather than sit on it.

EXERCISE:
COMMUNICATING YOUR TRANSFORMATION WITH CONVICTION

Now that you understand the importance of focusing on selling the tangible results your offers create, it's time to put it into practice. Follow these three simple steps to clarify and communicate the unparalleled transformation your offer delivers:

1. Define the Result

Write down the specific end result your offer delivers. Don't focus on the process or steps, instead, clearly describe the final transformation your clients experience.

Example: *"My clients multiply their revenue while gaining more time freedom."*

2. Rewrite Your Offer Statement Using Conviction-Led Language

Take your offer statement and rewrite it using conviction-led language. Make it clear, bold, and definitive. Leave no space for uncertainty.

Example: Instead of, "This program could help you increase your sales," say, "This program will help you 2X your sales within ninety days". Of course, you need to have the certainty and conviction that your offer can actually achieve this result if the client puts the work in.

3. Storytelling Time

Choose one client success story that highlights the transformation your offer delivered. Write it down, focusing on the journey from where they started to the incredible results they achieved. Keep it concise but impactful and make sure to communicate the emotions and tangible change your work created.

Example: *"Claire was struggling to close high-ticket clients and was feeling stuck with her income, unable to break through her £10k per month income ceiling. After working through the programme, she converted her first £20K client in just sixty days and scaled to six figures within six months. Now, she enjoys more financial freedom and flexibility with her time, so she can spend quality time with her family and children, without compromise."*

This exercise will help you articulate the life-changing transformation your offers create, using clear, conviction-led language and powerful storytelling to connect deeply with your ideal clients.

PILLAR SEVEN: MEANINGFUL UNIQUE MESSAGE

Your brand's unique message is the heart of your communication, marketing and sales strategy in your business and it sets the tone for your audience, i.e., how they perceive, interact and buy from you. It should differentiate you from competitors and resonate deeply with your audience. So, when it comes to your unique message, your job is to craft a message that speaks directly to your ideal, high-ticket clients, addressing their struggles, desires and the transformation you offer. It's about creating an emotional connection that goes beyond your offers, sales and marketing.

Your unique message needs to stand out and be differentiated from everyone else in your industry. It should differentiate your brand from your competitors and highlight what makes you unique. It requires you to speak to your ideal, high-ticket clients where they are at. It needs to recognise what their current struggles are, how this impacts them, their desires and ultimately, it needs to showcase that your work is the vehicle to solve their current problems and achieve their desires.

Remember, your brand essence is all about energy and feeling – it's how you make those who interact with your brand feel. By aligning your brand message and essence with the energy of your ideal client and their aspirations, you create a brand that not only stands out but also builds sustainable impact for your clients and long-term growth for your business.

EXERCISE: CRAFT YOUR MEANINGFUL UNIQUE MESSAGE

To help you create a unique brand message that resonates with your ideal high-ticket clients, follow these steps:

1. Identify Your Ideal Client's Struggles:
- Write down the top three struggles or challenges your ideal high-ticket client is currently facing.

Example: *"My clients struggle with feeling overwhelmed by scaling their business."*

2. Define Their Desired Outcome:
- Write down the key transformations or results they want from your offer.

Example: *"They want to experience more financial freedom and time to enjoy their life."*

3. Connect the Dots:
- Now, bridge the gap between their current struggles and the transformation your offer provides.
- Use this formula:
  "I help [ideal client] who are struggling with [specific problem] to achieve [desired transformation] through [your solution]."

Example: *"I help online coaches who feel overwhelmed by business growth to create sustainable six-figure months without sacrificing their personal time."*

4. Align with Emotion:

What emotion do you want to evoke when clients interact with your brand (e.g., empowerment, confidence, inspiration)?

Example: *"My brand evokes empowerment by showing clients they can scale their business with ease."*

5. Refine Your Message:

Combine all the above insights into a clear, compelling message that differentiates your brand. Make sure it's specific, emotionally driven and speaks to your unique approach.

Example: *"At [Brand Name], we empower online coaches to escape overwhelm and scale to six-figure months without burnout, using our proven [method] for business growth."*

FINAL STEP:

Now is a great time to test your new unique message by sharing it with a few trusted clients or peers for feedback. Ask them if it clearly conveys your brand's value and stands out from your competition.

As you conclude this part of your high-ticket journey and build your premium brand, remember that a truly magnetic brand is about much more than just visuals or a catchy tagline; it's about how you make people feel, the impact you create and the transformation you deliver. Your brand sets the stage but it's your message that amplifies your voice and attracts your ideal clients. In the next chapter, we'll dive deeper into crafting a powerful and compelling message that not only resonates with your audience but also positions you as the go-to expert for high-ticket clients in your industry. Ready to amplify your impact? Turn the page.

ACCESS YOUR EXCLUSIVE HIGH-TICKET MASTERY MINI-COURSE

Simply go to **bit.ly/Highticketmethodbookcourse** to access your Chapter Four resources and dive deeper into how to elevate your premium brand.

FIVE
YOUR MILLIONS ARE IN YOUR MESSAGING

I have a saying that I repeat to my clients consistently, and that is *"your millions are in your messaging"*. This essentially refers to identifying exactly which type of client you want to attract and work with. This requires you to get inside their head (not literally, of course) and understand exactly how they would describe their current struggle, how it impacts them in their life, the feelings they experience as a result and what life would feel like once they achieve their desired goal (what you help them do), using the exact language they would use when describing all of this to you in a hypothetical conversation and showcasing that you are the expert for them.

Tailoring your messaging to speak directly to your specific ideal client is essential. Your communication and message need to resonate with their specific needs and goals and what they're feeling and experiencing.

EXERCISE:
YOUR IDEAL, HIGH-TICKET CLIENT PERSONA

Here are some powerful prompts to help you identify your ideal high-ticket client persona to help bring this into your messaging:

1. What are the characteristics, pain points and aspirations of your dream, high-ticket clients?
2. How are these factors affecting them right now? What impact do their struggles have on their lives and emotions right now?

Your messaging should then position your offer as the non-negotiable solution to their problems. It's your job to make your offer stand out as the *only* solution they need. For example:

"You're currently at Point X [where they are now], but you want to reach Point Z [their goal/desire/aspiration]. This is the exact work we do together when you join me in Offer Y [your solution that bridges the gap from X to Z]."

Speaking only to your ideal, high-ticket client is key because if you don't, your sales and conversions will feel so much harder. If you speak specifically to your ideal client where they are at, the money and conversions will become easier. Bring this into your content and your content will start to do a lot of the heavy lifting for your client attraction and sales.

Here's the thing though, don't expect your ideal high-ticket clients to enquire about your work if you aren't specifically talking to them through your messaging. It's important to note here that this will take courage and, as previously explained using the Harrod's versus Co-op shop example, your job is to be brave and let go of needing to please all potential clients by trying to speak to everyone in your messaging. As you know, this results in attracting no one.

It's now time for you to decide to let go of playing small and it's time to play bigger than ever, focusing on attracting your ideal high-ticket client, the kind that jumps straight into your offers with a *"yes"*. It's time to step into your high-ticket expert identity.

I understand that you might be fighting with some mindset monkeys around this next step. It can feel scary to narrow your focus and speak directly to your ideal, high-ticket clients when you know how easy it is to convert your current clients. You might worry about excluding other potential clients or fear that you won't attract anyone at all and that you'll lose those clients to your cheaper competition. But remember, messaging to everyone often ends up attracting no one. It takes courage to be specific, but the rewards are exponential. When you confidently communicate your unique value, you'll attract those ideal clients who align perfectly with your vision and mission and who value your expertise.

I want you to remember that your high-value proposition makes you uniquely you and is what is going to differentiate you from everyone else who does the same as you in your industry. As a recap on what we've already covered, to do this, highlight the unique selling points of working with you and the transformational value you offer. Remember to emphasise the outcomes your work creates – the tangible end results, the ROI, the speed at which they could expect results when working with you inside your offer – and remember the four expert values – clients will pay you more if your high-ticket offer ticks all four expert values. Now is a good time to revisit the four expert values covered in Chapter Three.

WHO'S YOUR PERFECT MATCH?

High-ticket clients have specific criteria which you need to ensure you bring into your marketing and content to ensure your marketing efforts and messaging are speaking directly and specifically to this person, and not to the person you *think* you should be speaking to. It needs to be the perfect match.

Before I dive into the specific high-ticket client persona criteria, I need to reassure you that it is normal at this stage to feel a sense of impostor syndrome, self-sabotage or being your own harshest critic when it comes to speaking and messaging to a higher calibre of client.

This may be because you feel the results you are currently achieving in your business aren't enough for you to speak to the higher calibre client you desire to work with. You need to acknowledge and move on from this in order to speak to, attract and convert the higher-ticket clients you want to work with. Believe me, once you start attracting higher-ticket clients, business feels easier and more exciting and the results you create with your clients will be far beyond the results you are currently creating with your lower- and mid-ticket clients.

Once you take this leap of faith knowing that you and your existing results are enough, and you start speaking to the person you really want to work with, I guarantee you will wish you'd done it sooner, instead of deliberating over whether you are good enough, whether your current results are good enough and ultimately, whether you are worthy of serving a higher calibre client. The truth is that you are! If you've had these thoughts though, I want you to know that you are not alone. I often have clients who I could easily get in my head about not being good enough to serve. For example, I have clients with far bigger results than me in certain areas, such as their audience size and number of followers on social media. Some of my clients have 7X the audience size that I have. Now, I could very easily tell myself that I'm not worthy of serving these kinds of clients (who, by the way, are getting incredible results) because I don't have the social media followers that they do, however, I remind myself that they hire and pay me for my specific expertise and genius, which they themselves have not yet conquered, i.e., attracting higher-paying, faster-moving clients to elevate their impact and income.

So, this is your reminder to let go of feeling too small, to let go of not feeling good enough, to unleash yourself as the expert who gets paid high-ticket prices and to speak only to the higher-calibre clients you really want to work with. It's time to give yourself full permission for this.

YOUR IDEAL, HIGH-TICKET CLIENT CRITERIA

Let's now dive into the criteria of the high-ticket client persona:

First things first, high-ticket clients have or can find access to the finances needed to invest in your service. Now this specifically means that you therefore need to be messaging in your content and marketing to the client who already has money, i.e., not the one who is struggling.

This is a really good time for you to audit your messaging and content, to ensure that the ideal client you're currently messaging to is actually the ideal high-ticket client you want and not someone who is financially unable to invest in your services.

Secondly, high-ticket clients are already problem-aware. They are aware that they have a challenge, struggle or difficulty that they need help with solving. This means they need less educational content from you, explaining to them that they have a problem in the first place.

Thirdly, high-ticket clients are solution aware. As we now know, they are already aware they have a problem that needs solving, but they are now also aware that they need help and support to achieve the solution to their problem. This is where you and your offer come in as the only solution to resolving their problem.

To illustrate this concept, let's consider a person walking through the nature-filled, green fields of the English countryside. As they stroll along, they enjoy the vibrant scenery, unaware that they will soon encounter a river they need to cross. At this point, they are unaware of their problem. However, when they reach the riverbank, they suddenly recognise the challenge and problem ahead: they need to cross the river to get to the other side. They need a bridge. At this point, they are problem-aware.

It's far easier for them to accept the necessity of the bridge as the solution to their problem once they face the river directly than it would be to convince them of its importance while they're still in the fields, blissfully unaware of the impending problem of the river that needs crossing.

This analogy directly applies to your business. When your ideal clients are aware of their problem and understand that they need a solution, it becomes much easier for you to position your offer as the only solution to their dilemma. It also requires less time and effort on your part to educate them that they have a problem which needs solving and then to subsequently sell your offer.

The fourth criterion of high-ticket clients is powerful — they need zero convincing or persuading to invest in your offer. Identify your ideal, high-ticket client, speak to them specifically and directly in your messaging and your content and marketing will do the heavy lifting when it comes to your sales. Sales will feel easier. Conversions will happen faster. You will speed up the buying process from someone landing on your social media accounts or website to buying from you as a paying customer. Do this really well and this exact process could happen on day one of them finding you.

What this means for you and your high-ticket messaging and marketing is that you need to move away from convincing and persuasive language and start implementing language which is authority-led and positions your high-ticket offer as the only solution to their problem.

EXAMPLE:

Instead of saying:

"This offer could help you achieve X if you put in the effort and commit to the process."

Use:

"When you join this program, and if you're ready to do the work, you'll confidently achieve X, because this system has already transformed the businesses and lives of clients just like you. This is the proven solution you've been looking for to get you from [their current pain point] to [their desired outcome]."

This shift in language moves from tentative and convincing to confident and certain, positioning your high-ticket offer as the undeniable solution.

The fifth key trait of your ideal high-ticket client persona is that they are self-driven. This specifically means they don't need you to hold their hand throughout the buying process. Once they've decided to work with you, they are in. There may be a few questions here or there, which is to be expected, but they will already have decided that you are the expert for them. Your content and marketing will have done the heavy lifting for you. What this means for you and your high-ticket messaging and marketing, is that you need to make it clear that your offers are for the self-led, fast-moving client, not someone who deliberates for days or weeks over an investment decision.

Lastly, the final criterion of a high-ticket client is that it is very likely that they understand investments. They are very likely accustomed to investing in their self-development, their business and even wealth-building assets. What this means for you and your messaging is that to attract this calibre of client, you need to remember to speak about the outcomes, tangible results and ROI which your offer will create for them, and not focus on the price or process involved as previously covered. You need less convincing and educating around the fact that working with you is an investment for a result, rather than a cost, to attract this kind of client.

EXERCISE:
HERE'S A CHECKLIST OF KEY ELEMENTS TO KEEP IN MIND WHEN CRAFTING YOUR HIGH-TICKET MESSAGING AND MARKETING CONTENT.

Your High-Ticket Messaging Checklist:

- **Have a client-centric approach:** Make your marketing all about them, not about you. When you make it all about them, you'll witness a significant increase in both impact and income.

- **Exclusivity and personalisation:** Highlight how your offers are bespoke and tailored to meet the specific needs of each client.

- **Establish authority and thought leadership:** As you already know, clients need to feel your authority and leadership for the certainty that you are the expert for them.

- **Use power language:** Opt for certain, assertive language instead of possibility language. This creates a stronger impression of confidence and reliability.

- **Foster genuine relationships:** Focus your marketing efforts on creating genuine deep relationships via personalised connections and bespoke solutions. Your marketing should reflect a client-focused mindset that values relationship-building.

- **Detach from the outcome:** This is my all-time favourite. High-ticket clients buy in their own time and are often not influenced by urgency or scarcity tactics, so bear this in mind. When someone is so attached and dependent on the outcome of a sale, it screams desperation. This is something you need to avoid. We'll explore this further in Chapter Ten when we dive into premium sales strategies.

> "STOP THE CHASE AND ATTACHMENT TO THE OUTCOME. EMBRACE DETACHMENT FROM THE OUTCOME. THIS COMES FROM YOUR INNER KNOWING THAT IT WILL HAPPEN. IT'S LIKE A MUSCLE – IT'S NOT EASY AT FIRST BUT THE MORE YOU PRACTICE AND TRAIN IT, THE EASIER THIS WILL BE."
>
> — TANIA KING-MOHAMMAD

While it's important for me to tell you exactly what key elements to include in your high-ticket messaging, it's also important for me to highlight what not to include.

The first is that we are not focused as such on the volume of clients. Remember that we are focused on attracting and converting a specific, higher-calibre client, which means speaking only to them, not to everyone. Remember, Harrods aren't scared of losing out on business by speaking to a tiny percentage of their total potential audience. You shouldn't be either.

Your marketing should never be about affordability because this won't resonate with your ideal, high-ticket clients. Never assume what they can or can't afford — have you ever lied to a salesperson before? Okay, so, you know where I'm coming from. The antithesis to my last point about what you should include in your marketing is to stay away from any attachment to the outcome of a sale. Nothing is more off-putting than someone desperate for a sale.

MAGNETIC MESSAGING THAT FLOODS YOUR INBOX WITH ENQUIRIES

When crafting your messaging, marketing and content, your mission is to make every piece irresistibly magnetic, amplifying and elevating both your impact and sales. To do this and to multiply your conversions faster than ever, it's your job to elevate your ideal high-ticket buyers to feel something because people buy from emotion and not logic. You now know that your ideal premium buyers need to see confidence and certainty in you, as the expert, to buy quickly from you, so make sure this comes through in your marketing.

High-ticket clients need assurance that you have high levels of confidence in them achieving the results and ROI they desire by working with you. Your ideal clients also need to feel your sense of authority because this demonstrates that you know your stuff and are worthy of a high-ticket investment. As we've already discussed, they need to identify with you, your content and your current client journeys because this shows them that your clients' results could be theirs too. To do this effectively, bring in storytelling content as a big piece of your marketing plan. There is no better strategy than storytelling content to build real connections.

> "YOU'LL MAKE MORE SALES WHEN YOU MAKE
> EVERYTHING YOU DO IN BUSINESS ALL ABOUT
> YOUR CLIENTS AND NOTHING ABOUT YOU."
>
> — TANIA KING-MOHAMMAD

Your message and content should be about intentionally creating an emotional connection that goes far beyond your offers, sales and marketing. Remember that people buy from how you make them feel, so make it all about them and not about you. Your bank balance will thank you for this.

MAGNETIC MESSAGING

The key to attracting, activating and converting those ideal, high-ticket clients, ready and waiting to pay you top-dollar, is understanding exactly what makes you stand out. The answer to this is the unique system or method which you use to teach your subject, which we've covered in Chapter Four. There will be hundreds and thousands of people teaching, coaching, consulting and mentoring on the same subject as you. Not many people are teaching new, ground-breaking strategies anymore because they've mostly all been taught. Teaching value-led information won't cut through the noise and get you paid anymore. Let's face it, nearly every strategy under the sun today is 'Googleable'. What does work, though, is the unique way in which *you* teach your commonly taught subject.

Your ideal, high-ticket clients are looking for an expert who teaches your subject in a unique way, using a unique angle, method or system. If you talk in the same way about the same stuff as all of the other hundreds or thousands of people doing exactly what you do, you'll attract the same clients as everyone else – you won't cut through the noise. There'll be no 'X-factor', no 'secret sauce'. And as we know, there is a lot of noise in the online space. You want to step into your next level and own your uniqueness by crafting your unique angle and method to teach your subject. Once you've figured out what that is, start shouting about it from the rooftops.

Now is your time to think carefully about what your unique angle and method are. The work we will do now will build on what we've already covered in Chapter Four.

KEY MAGNETIC MESSAGING TIPS

Here are my key magnetic messaging tips to attract, activate and convert your ideal high-ticket clients:

- Be as specific as possible when it comes to speaking only to your dream, ideal client in every piece of content.

- Speak using the second person in your content – it's all about *'you'* and not about *'we'*, *'they'* or *'one'* — make it *all* about them.

- Speak to your ideal client's desires more than their pain points. By using traditional 'pain point marketing', you increase the distance between where your ideal client is now and where they want to be, instead of activating them to move and invest in your services. By utilising 'desire-led marketing', you bring your ideal client closer to where they want to be, making it feel more possible for them to achieve their desires and therefore raising the probability of them investing in your offer.

- Be bold. Demonstrate your leadership and don't be scared to give value. So many people shy away from overdelivering value because they're scared that clients then won't convert. In fact, what actually happens is people get a taste of the results they can get from working with you, leaving them wanting more.

- Give more value than your competition. This is a key unique selling point and should apply to everything you do, from your free offers and content to your high-ticket containers and experiences. The more tangible value you give at each level, the more your impact and income will soar.

- Showcase your unique method and angle for what you do across your marketing.

- Always create content relating to the offer which you are selling. By consistently referring to your offers in your content, you increase the awareness your audience has of what you have to offer and therefore their likeliness to buy.

- Avoid possibility language and use powerful conviction-led vocabulary to help activate and move your ideal, high-ticket buyers.

- Keep each piece of content specific by focusing on solving one key problem per piece of content. Don't overload and overwhelm your audience by trying to solve multiple problems in one post. It won't work. It will confuse your audience and your sales will be impacted.

As we wrap up this chapter on messaging that is magnetic, the key takeaway I want you to remember is this: your millions are in your messaging. The more precisely you define who you're speaking to in your marketing and the more clearly you address where they are now (not where you think they are), while positioning your offer as the must-have solution to achieve their desired result, the faster and easier it becomes to attract, engage and convert your ideal, high-ticket clients.

Your messaging is one of your most powerful tools so use it to create the impact and income you want.

ACCESS YOUR EXCLUSIVE HIGH-TICKET MASTERY MINI-COURSE

Simply go to **bit.ly/Highticketmethodbookcourse** to access your Chapter Five resources and dive deeper into how to create magnetic messaging and marketing.

SIX
YOUR IRRESISTIBLE HIGH-TICKET POWER OFFER

Welcome to Chapter Six, where things really start to heat up! This is where we'll dive into creating your next, irresistible, high-ticket power offer that will get the attention of your ideal, high-ticket clients and position you as the go-to expert for high-ticket clients in your industry.

YOUR POWER OFFER

When I talk about creating an *"irresistible high-ticket offer"* I'm referring to what I call your **"POWER offer"**. Your power offer is an offer unlike anyone else's in your niche and industry and stands out far and wide from anything else available on the market.

The moment you come to think about creating your high-ticket power offer, I want you to put yourself into the shoes of your ideal, high-ticket client and imagine them saying, *"Make me an offer I can't refuse"*. This will instantly elevate your excitement, creativity and potential around creating your new irresistible offer, making you instantly think about the extra value and support to include in your power offer and the elevated transformations you want to help co-create with it.

First, though, we need to shift your mindset from wanting to sell all of your offers to anyone in your audience to being intentional about the specific clients you want to work with, and how to make these offers irresistible.

WHY OFFERS DON'T SELL

I have endless conversations with entrepreneurs in the online space who have the most incredible offers that would genuinely change lives and businesses. However, I consistently hear that, for whatever reason, these offers simply aren't selling. If you find yourself in this boat, I want you to know that you are not alone and I want you to know, that you're in exactly the right place to fix this as there is work we can do on this to make sure your offers do sell out, and that they are being bought by your ideal, high-ticket clients.

The reason these incredible offers aren't selling out is that there are so many people in every niche talking about and selling the same thing. I know you're here to make extraordinary money by multiplying your impact and income through working with high-ticket clients and you want to learn how to do this the right way, by creating a huge impact. However, the reality is that if you sell ordinary offers for an ordinary price, you will make ordinary money.

There is just too much of the same old thing on the market. When we bring it back to the classic supply and demand curve, there simply isn't enough demand to sell out your offers if they're the same or similar to everyone else, because there's lots of a similar thing and therefore a high supply. By selling a similar offer to everyone else in your niche, you aren't standing out from the crowd or giving yourself the opportunity to maximise your earning potential.

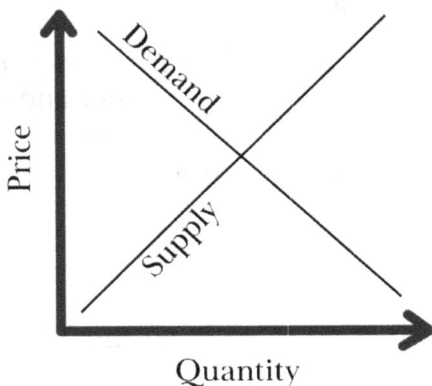

KNOW YOUR MARKET

The first thing you need to do is to audit your competition. Have a look at their content and marketing and identify what messaging they are using. Who are they speaking to? And how are they speaking to them? Have a look at exactly what they are selling. Identify the key elements of their high-ticket offers – the duration, what's included, the end result and ROI and, of course, the price point. Ask yourself who their high-ticket offer is specifically designed for.

Now ask yourself how they have optimised their offer. By this, I mean look specifically at any bonuses or incentives they have added in, such as closer proximity to them or their team and start to think what you could add in too, which you currently haven't. This is your opportunity to take notes because I need you to be ten steps ahead. I need you to think and act bigger. Go the extra mile with the value you deliver, and you will create the extra impact and get paid the extra money. You'll understand exactly what I mean as we progress through this chapter.

Now look at your market and ask yourself how many people in your niche are selling a premium or high-ticket offer. It's unlikely not many and certainly not as many as the number of experts selling low- and mid-ticket offers. The reason for this is that it is much easier to commit to selling at the lower-ticket price points in the lower-ticket brackets. The only problem here is that you don't reap the financial results unless you have a huge and engaged audience where your financial results are based on volume. That's not the game that we want to play. Remember, we want to sell specific, bespoke, high-ticket offers to specific and select high-ticket clients. This is not a volume game.

THE POWER OF EXCLUSIVITY PSYCHOLOGY

Take a moment to look at your market and ask yourself how many people in your niche are truly offering premium or high-ticket services. Now, imagine the transformation in your business and client relationships once you start selling a high-ticket offer. You would elevate your demand, skyrocket your clients' results and significantly boost the perceived value of your brand and offers. You'll also tap into a powerful psychological tool: exclusivity.

Exclusivity enhances your brand's perceived value and creates a sense of desire for your high-ticket services. It signals that your offer isn't for everyone and the more you embrace this strategy in your marketing, the more you'll attract affluent clients looking for unique, tailored experiences which they are prepared to pay high-ticket prices for. By making your offer exclusive, you elevate the sense of scarcity, desirability and prestige — ultimately attracting clients who are ready and willing to invest at the highest level. Cha-ching!

WHAT MAKES A POWER OFFER POWERFUL?

Your power offer is your ticket to getting paid more for the work that you love, without multiplying your workload. A power offer is one where you provide more value, resources and, usually, closer proximity support with you or your team. It helps distinguish your offer from the other offers available in your niche. It's an offer which has a higher perceived value attached to it compared to the other offers available in your market. By creating and selling a power offer, you can drive buying decisions that are based on value and results rather than price. It's an irresistible offer that your ideal, high-ticket clients can't refuse.

What takes a power offer from merely being a *"nice-to-have"* choice to a *"must-have"* necessity is its ability to stand out as non-negotiable in a plethora of options within your niche. A powerful offer is not just differentiated; it's value-packed and irresistibly appealing to your ideal, high-ticket clients. To achieve this, you must enhance your offer by including bonuses and added support and resources, clearly communicating the results and ROI your clients can expect and emphasising the world-class value delivered.

This approach shifts your pricing strategy from just listing features to focusing on the value and outcomes associated with your offer. A power offer is always in demand, consistently sought after by your ideal, high-ticket clients. It embodies the four essential expert values discussed earlier in this book: it enhances client results, accelerates their path to success, simplifies the journey towards their goals and mitigates the risks of wasted time and finances. By demonstrating that your power offer meets these criteria, you create an irresistible, high-ticket offer that will practically fly off the shelves.

THE SECRET BEHIND HIGH-IMPACT POWER OFFERS

The foundation of a power offer lies in its commitment to service and value. This principle starts with your free content, lead magnets and so on. Don't fall into the trap that many entrepreneurs do by offering generic freebies and low-value content just because it's not generating much or any revenue. If you're serious about building a pipeline of strong, qualified leads who will eventually convert into paying clients, you need to raise the bar across everything you deliver, including your free stuff.

Instead of following the crowd, ask yourself, *"How can I ensure that my free, low-, mid-, or high-ticket offers are truly value-packed?"* Consider how you can provide support and deliver results that exceed anything else available in your niche. By focusing on exceptional value at every level, you'll attract clients who recognise the value of your services and who are ready to invest in your services.

For example, my **Five-Day Free High-Ticket Sprint** has generated thousands in new sales in just five days for our participants. While this experience is free, the significant results produced during such a short time period elevate its perceived value. It demonstrates that engaging with this free experience can lead to a high return on investment on one's time, making it clear to my audience that participating is worth their time.

The more value you give at every level in your product suite, starting from the free stuff, the more trust you build and the more time you collapse between a new follower finding you and then becoming a paying client. You speed up the buying process. To be able to do this and make sure that your offer stands out in terms of value, support and results as mentioned earlier in this chapter, you need to know what else is available in your niche. This knowledge enables you to overdeliver and really differentiate your offer, making it irresistible to your ideal clients.

THE POWER OFFER FRAMEWORK

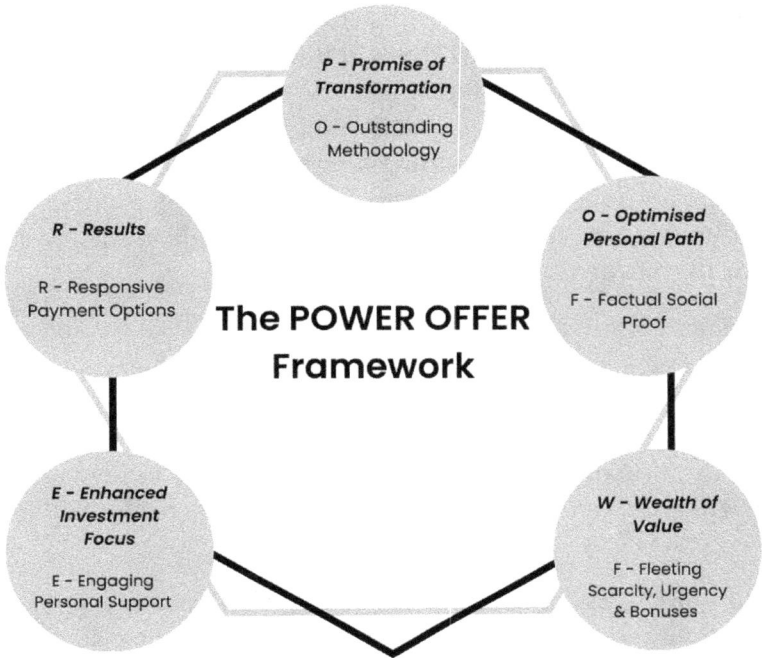

The power offer framework is the ten-step system I take my clients through to help them create irresistible high-ticket offers that sell. It's built on specificity where you speak to one, specific, ideal, high-ticket client, it creates a high-ticket offer which resolves a specific problem and supports your clients in achieving their specific desired results. Ultimately, the power framework creates a high-ticket offer that's irresistible to your ideal high-ticket clients. This ten-step framework outlines the core elements of an irresistible high-ticket offer. It's a step-by-step process designed to help you create a compelling high-ticket offer that not only captures the attention of the premium buyers you want to work with but also drives sales. Below, I'll take you through each step, in detail, ensuring that you have everything you need to create your next irresistible, high-ticket power offer.

P – Promise of Transformation

To craft a powerful promise of transformation for your offer — one that sells quickly and effortlessly — you need to be crystal clear on who your ideal client is. Seriously, take the time to nail down your specific, high-ticket client persona before diving into this step. Trust me; this groundwork is essential which is why I'm mentioning it again. If you don't have this nailed down, nothing else you try to add on top will work.

When you're communicating the promise and transformation of your power offer, tailor your unique methodology to meet your ideal client's needs and desires. Show them that your power offer is the ultimate formula to bridge the gap between where they are now and where they want to be.

Demonstrate the transformative outcomes and tangible results possible for them once they implement your offer. It's your responsibility to highlight the specific positive changes they can look forward to from implementing your service or offer. This isn't just about selling; it's about igniting them to take action by showing them the incredible results that they too could create.

O – Optimised Personal Path

This step encourages you to create a unique system which enables you to assess your individual client needs and then tailor your offer and experience accordingly. You therefore need to recognise your ideal clients' unique strengths, weaknesses and goals and then showcase how your offer and support can adapt to their individual needs to achieve their desired results.

W – Wealth of Value

In this step, it's time to dive deep and list every single struggle your ideal client faces. Your power offer needs to address each and every one of these challenges head-on. Think about how this could manifest: maybe you design different modules that tackle each struggle, or perhaps you include bonuses and extra resources. You might even add personalised, bespoke support to create a more intimate experience.

Once you have this foundation, your next job is to showcase the immense value your clients will receive, not just in terms of the content and features of your offer, but also regarding the personal growth, mindset shifts and tangible results they can achieve and celebrate from the wealth of value packed into your power offer.

It's important to exceed the expectations of your audience and ideal clients when it comes to delivering value. Think about how you can elevate their experience! This might mean incorporating additional bonuses or exclusive experiences, such as the luxury retreat I host each year as part of my Wealthy Mastermind. Alternatively, consider bringing in associate mentors or coaches to enrich your programme. Even simple enhancements like providing extra resources can make a significant impact.

Make sure to create a detailed outline that clearly explains all the value and support included at each stage of your offer. This not only ensures that you're delivering an exceptional experience, but it also aligns perfectly with your client's needs and desires. By going above and beyond, you'll create a power offer that stands out and resonates personally with your ideal clients.

E – Enhanced Investment Focus

This step of the power offer framework is all about clearly communicating the ROI that your offer delivers and aims to provide. Your job is to emphasise how your clients' high-ticket investment leads to significant, long-term benefits. It's not just about paying for a service, it's about investing in a transformative result. To highlight this, show them how their investment in your power offer will drive the exact outcomes they're seeking.

To encourage and drive the investment focus for your clients inside your offer, it's important to operate a system for tracking your client progress, collecting testimonials and showcasing the tangible results which can be achieved. This not only encourages potential clients to see the value in investing but also strengthens your credibility, making it easier for them to trust that your offer is worth it.

R – Results

This step is all about showcasing the proven results that your offer delivers. Use case studies, testimonials and success stories to clearly communicate the tangible outcomes your clients have achieved. By highlighting real-life examples of transformation, you're demonstrating the effectiveness of your offer and giving your ideal, high-ticket clients confidence that they can achieve similar results. This is where your offer moves from being theoretical to something concrete, backed by real evidence of success.

O – Outstanding Methodology

As we've already covered, the most powerful way to stand out in your niche is by creating your own unique methodology. Your specific system or framework sets you apart as the authority in your field. For example, this book walks you through my six-step system, *The High-Ticket Method*®, designed to attract high-ticket clients and multiply your impact and income. As I have already advised, if you don't already have your own methodology, now's the time to create it. Outline the steps you take your clients through and give it a memorable name. Use client success stories to show how your methodology delivers results, reinforcing your credibility and expertise.

F – Factual Social Proof

This step is all about leveraging the power of your client testimonials and success stories to sell your power offer. Sharing real-life results from past or current clients builds credibility and trust and shows that your offer delivers. Factual social proof makes your offer irresistible by demonstrating its value through the successes of others, which reassures potential clients that they, too, can achieve similar results.

F – Fleeting Scarcity, Urgency and Bonuses

This is where you can really optimise your power offer, but there's a crucial caveat: only use scarcity, urgency and bonuses with integrity. If you set a deadline for clients to buy, stick to it. If you offer a time-limited bonus, make sure it's genuinely time-limited.

While these tactics have developed a bad reputation in some circles, when used appropriately, they can be powerful activators helping your ideal clients to make informed decisions when it comes to investing. They help clients take decisive action to achieve their desired outcomes, especially if hesitation has been holding them back. The key is to use these elements intentionally, to add value, enhance results and create genuine change. When used with integrity, they can be highly effective tools that inspire clients to commit to achieving the results they want. Note: As I've previously mentioned, not all high-ticket clients respond to urgency or scarcity tactics, so it's important to use them carefully and with consideration. These elements should enhance your offer without feeling forced and focus on delivering value and serving your clients at the highest level possible.

E – Engaging Personal Support

At this step, I encourage my clients to highlight the level of personal support and attention their clients will receive by investing in their power offer. To ensure this is consistently delivered, it's crucial to create systems that facilitate regular communication, provide ongoing support and guarantee a personalised experience for each client. This ensures you're not just promising but also delivering an exceptional, high-touch service.

R – Responsive Payment Options.

For a long time, I avoided offering payment plans in my business, however, I now strongly encourage implementing flexible payment options where possible. These options make it easier for clients to invest in your offer, expanding your impact and accessibility. From a business perspective, this is a game-changer in building your monthly recurring revenue (MRR), which is your guaranteed income from clients on subscriptions or payment plans.

If you're aiming for consistent multi-five or six-figure months, you can't afford to start from zero at the beginning of each month. Having a reliable MRR provides a stable foundation to build upon each month. If you've hesitated about using payment plans, now is the time to start — just be sure you have the proper legal contracts in place to protect both your business and your clients.

EXERCISE:
CRAFTING YOUR IRRESISTIBLE HIGH-TICKET POWER OFFER

As you create your power offer, take a moment to revisit the key criteria of a high-ticket client we discussed in Chapter Five. This will ensure your offer is tailored specifically for your ideal high-ticket client.

Remember, high-ticket clients are driven by the transformation they want to achieve, moving them from point A to point B. They're not interested in the process itself, they want the end results. Think of my famous analogy: people buy the beach body, not the gym routine. Your role is to showcase how your power offer will get them there.

Step One: Reverse Engineer the End Result

What is the ultimate result your ideal, high-ticket client wants to achieve? Consider the timeframe in which your power offer can help them attain this result. Outline how you will deliver your power offer and identify the steps, tools and strategies your clients need for success.

Step Two: Amplify the Value

Next, think about how to enhance your offer to make it stand out from the competition in your niche. Focus on delivering the four expert values: bigger results, speed of results, convenience and reduced risk.

You have the power to decide right now if you want to create ordinary offers with ordinary impact and income, or extraordinary offers that lead to extraordinary results. It all takes just one decision.

As we conclude Chapter Six, I hope you can now see that crafting an irresistible, high-ticket POWER offer is not just about making a sale, it's about creating a transformative experience for your clients. Remember, bringing exclusivity and world-class value into your offers is your secret weapon behind standing out in a crowded market. Now, armed with the strategies we've discussed, it's time to put your learnings into action.

ACCESS YOUR EXCLUSIVE HIGH-TICKET MASTERY MINI-COURSE

Simply go to **bit.ly/Highticketmethodbookcourse** to access your Chapter Six resources and dive deeper into how to create your POWER offer.

SEVEN
YOUR PROFITABLE HIGH-TICKET PRODUCT SUITE

Your profitable product suite is the key to ensuring you never leave money on the table. Get it right and you provide a home for your clients which means that you multiply your impact and income to the next level by attracting high-ticket clients who stay in your world longer.

Now is the time to unlock the true earning potential of your business by implementing the power of a high-ticket product suite. This isn't just about price points; this is your commitment to delivering unparalleled value, an investment in deeper impact for your clients and a gateway to extraordinary results, not just for you, but for your clients too.

YOUR BUSINESS MODEL – YOUR LIFE, YOUR BUSINESS: BUILD YOUR LIFE AND BUSINESS BY DESIGN

Your key to building a sustainable business which generates long-term results and grows consistently, without you always having to operate within the business is to build your business by design. What I mean by this is, when it comes to designing your business model, first start with identifying the lifestyle, the freedom and the location that you want to have and live in and *then* design the business model to accommodate this lifestyle for you this is building a life and business by design.

To build your life and business by design, be really honest with yourself and identify the lifestyle that you genuinely want. This also means recognising your strengths, values and the ways you thrive in your work. Consider the types of programmes you want to deliver — whether that's live trainings, pre-recorded sessions or a mix of both — and the launch styles that resonate with you.

Most importantly, identify what brings you the most joy, both in life and business, and explore how you can incorporate these elements into the fabric of your life and the business which you are building. Ask yourself what key aspects you want to include in your business because they energise you. And just as crucially, be honest about what you definitely want to avoid. This self-awareness is the foundation for creating a life and business that aligns with your true self, paving the way for fulfilment and the results you want.

YOUR PROFITABLE PRODUCT SUITE

Let's dive into the different levels of offers that you can include in your profitable product suite and how to differentiate the access to you, client results and your pricing structure.

Your product suite should consist of high-, mid-, and low-ticket offers. Having all three is important to ensure you're maximising your revenue and not leaving any money on the table. This is because each level plays a unique role: high-ticket offers provide in-depth transformation and close proximity personal support; mid-ticket offers offer valuable resources and guidance; and low-ticket offers serve as your accessible entry points for your potential clients.

We'll explore how to craft these offers effectively and optimise your sales strategy later in this chapter.

HIGH-TICKET OFFERS

Let's start with your high ticket offers. These will generally be offers, experiences or programmes where your clients get more close proximity to you during and outside of your coaching, mentoring or consulting sessions with them. This means, your clients get more of your time and there will likely be a significant one-to-one element. Because high-ticket offers require more of your time, there is going to be a client number ceiling on how many high-ticket clients can join certain high-ticket offers of yours at any one time.

When considering high-ticket offers for your business model, think about options like one-to-one support, masterminds, retreats and VIP days. These offers provide your clients with the closest proximity to you, making them your highest-priced options.

Keep in mind that price points for high-ticket offers can vary widely depending on the individual and business model. For instance, I've seen individuals charging £100,000 for a year of one-to-one support, while others set their prices between £5,000 and £20,000. It's important not to get caught up in what constitutes a *"high-ticket"* price for you. What matters is finding a price point that feels right for you and reflects the support, value and results you deliver to your clients. Focus on what feels authentic and sustainable for your business and ensure it's at a price which you can energetically back.

MID-TICKET OFFERS

With mid-ticket offers, there may be an element of one-to-one support; however, there is much less close proximity to you than in your high-ticket offers. This means your clients will get less one-to-one time with you. Some mid-ticket offers will have no one-to-one element at all. Again, decide on the business model you want to build based on the lifestyle you want to live. Examples of mid-ticket offers could include group programmes where you are delivering to many clients at the same time (meaning there is no client number ceiling on the number of clients that can join these offers), live events, virtual events, digital assets, DIY self-study courses, mid-ticket memberships and VIP days. Generally speaking, I would class a mid-ticket offer as anything priced between £500-£5000. Again, this will vary according to each individual.

LOW-TICKET OFFERS

Low-ticket offers are still an essential part of your profitable product suite. I don't want you to think that because my area of expertise is high-ticket client attraction and sales, that low- and mid-ticket sales don't play a part in a hugely profitable product suite, because they absolutely do. Low-ticket offers are those which deliver no proximity to you. There is no one-to-one coaching element and there will be little to none of your time delivered. As a result, there is no ceiling on the number of clients that can join these offers because your time in client delivery doesn't change with the number of clients that come into these offers. The exciting thing is that these offers can also be completely passive or semi-passive.

Examples of low-ticket offers you can incorporate into your product suite include masterclasses (whether live or pre-recorded), low-ticket memberships, micro-offers and DIY self-study courses. I typically define low-ticket offers as anything priced up to £500. These options allow you to engage a broader audience while still providing valuable content and transformations. By diversifying your offers, you create multiple touchpoints for potential clients to interact with your brand, paving the way for them to eventually invest in your higher-ticket services as they progress along your client pathway, also known as a client ascension ladder.

To conclude this section on your business model, I want to share some golden pointers to help you take action without feeling overwhelmed and ending in you taking no action. First and foremost, don't get overwhelmed thinking that you need to do all of this at once. Focus on building one block in your business at a time. Don't look at the mountain from the outset, look at the small consistent steps you can take that compound, over time, into big results.

I want you to focus on creating and launching one offer in your product suite at a time so that you don't spread yourself too thin. This way, you get to build awareness around that specific offer, and you build a reputation for that signature offer. And with every offer you create, always be mindful of how you want your lifestyle and, therefore, your business model to look in the future. Be mindful to always reverse engineer from that place first.

DESIGNING YOUR PROFITABLE PRODUCT SUITE: MULTIPLY YOUR IMPACT AND INCOME

The power of having a profitable product suite in your business is that you simply have a solution for everyone in your audience in terms of where they are in their journey, what support they need at each stage and their financial accessibility. Simply, you have somewhere for everyone to go who wants to work with you. This means that you stop leaving money on the table and you always have something to offer each potential client no matter where they are in their journey or their finances.

From a business and income-generating perspective, establishing a profitable product suite is vital for maximising your client lifetime value (CLV). CLV represents the total financial value of each client over the duration of their relationship with your business. By offering a range of offers and services, you can encourage clients to engage with multiple offers, thereby increasing their lifetime value and boosting your revenue. Additionally, a well-structured product suite enhances the stability, security and sustainability of your business. It enables you to consistently convert and onboard new clients, driving the ongoing growth you want and elevating your revenue potential.

The key takeaway here is that if you're solely focused on selling a single offer, you're potentially leaving thousands of pounds in unclaimed sales on the table and limiting the impact you could have on many more clients. Now is the time to start mapping out your lifestyle and business model by design, along with the profitable product suite that you need to support this vision and make it your reality.

HIGH-TICKET OFFER SUITES

Product suites that embrace high-ticket offers are structured differently from those focused primarily on low- and mid-ticket offers or services. As you know, the goal of a high-ticket product suite is to justify your higher price points by delivering world-class value and a comprehensive solution tailored to address your ideal high clients' specific needs and desires. This means providing the right support and expertise that transforms their challenges into lasting results.

You will need a core signature high-ticket offer which will be your flagship signature offer, typically priced at the highest point in your product suite. This high-ticket offer, as you now know from the power offer framework, should provide a wealth of value and directly address a major pain point and/or desire for your ideal, high-ticket clients.

To multiply your income and elevate your client lifetime value, you will need to offer additional products or services that complement the core signature offer, which are known as up-sells, down-sells and add-ons. These could be advanced features, extended support, exclusive access or premium add-ons which are designed and delivered to enhance the overall value and amplify the result your client achieves within your high-ticket offer.

OFFER SUITE COMPONENTS

Your profitable product suite will include multiple offers, so ensuring alignment and complementarity among them is important. Make this process obvious and straightforward. Once a client enters your world and business ecosystem, it's your responsibility to keep them engaged and connected as a client. You can only do this with a suitable, profitable product suite already in place.

Things to consider here and make this happen, are that your clients' needs, knowledge and goals are constantly evolving. Their financial status is constantly evolving. The degree of proximity that they will want with you is also evolving. Someone may come into your lowest offer at the beginning of their journey with you with the aim to move up into your mid-ticket and then your highest-paid offer once they are further along their journey and once their financial status permits them to do so. Your job, therefore, is to have offers which can support your ideal clients at every stage to accommodate all of these dynamic and changing factors. You need to evolve with them and be able to offer the appropriate support that they need at every level of business, with the various levels of proximity that they may want, through the various containers and experiences that you offer.

It's your job to create opportunities for your clients to stay in your world – make it easy and obvious for them to stick around, and they will! It costs much more in time and money invested to source new audiences and new clients than it does to retain and sell to your existing audience and clients. So, as I always advise my clients, focus on the key activities in your business that generate your biggest ROI when it comes to your time and finances. I'll show you exactly how to retain your ideal, high-ticket clients in your business in my **'Clients-and-Cash-on-Repeat System'** in Chapter Nine. You're going to love it.

EXERCISE: YOUR ESSENTIAL CHECKLIST FOR BUILDING A PROFITABLE PRODUCT SUITE

Below is a really useful checklist of things for you to think about when building your profitable product suite so that you create one which delivers all required components at each stage of the client journey:

- **Client Experience:** What type of experience do you want to deliver?
- **Price Point:** What will be the pricing strategy for each offer?
- **Level of Support:** What level of support is required at each stage?
- **Client Assessment:** Where is your client currently? What do they need now and in the future?
- **Retention Motivation:** Why would clients want to continue working with you?
- **Growth Support:** How can you support your ideal clients as they evolve beyond their current offer?
- **Desired Experience:** What experience do your ideal clients want at each stage?
- **Proximity:** What level of access do your ideal clients want and need from you?
- **Time Commitment:** What is the time investment required for each offering?
- **Scalable Offers:** What additional scalable offers can you introduce that require less of your time and have

no client number ceiling?

- **Consistent Sales:** How can you generate more consistent sales across your suite?

THE ONE-TO-MORE SYSTEM

The one-to-more system is the three-step system I teach my clients to follow when building out their profitable product suites. My advice is to always start with a signature, high-ticket offer such as a one-to-one offer. As you know, this is not a scalable offer because it requires you to exchange your time for money. There is a limit to the number of clients you can have in these offers. However, by using the one-to-more system, with your experience, time in your niche, the growth and elevated engagement of your audience and your client results, you are then able to add scalable offers into your product suite. At this stage, when your signature, highest-ticket offer is sold out, in high demand and generating good client results, it is time to add in the second level of offer using the one-to-more system.

The second level offer to add in would be a one-to-many offer such as a group programme or mastermind. These one-to-many offers are scalable because unless you want one, there is no limit on the number of clients that can join them. This means that the more your audience grows and the more your reputation as the leading expert in your industry grows, I more people will join your one-to-many scalable offers, therefore growing your revenue as a result.

The third and final step in the one-to-more system is to add in other lower-cost scalable offers, such as self-led DIY courses, lower ticket memberships and so on. However, these will only launch and sell successfully when you have a larger and more engaged audience and when your stage one and two offers are already selling well.

As you progress through the three steps of the one-to-more system, your business becomes scalable, you generate more revenue and, importantly, you generate more monthly recurring revenue which gives you the solid foundation you need to achieve higher money months and revenue in your business.

THE ONE TO MORE SYSTEM

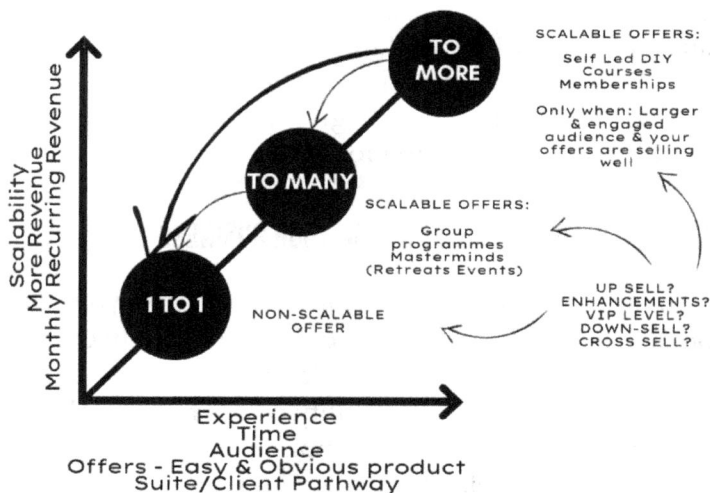

SCALING YOUR BUSINESS

Until you achieve consistent five-figure months and beyond in your business, I recommend focusing on selling your high-ticket signature offer alongside a signature group offer. This approach provides the flexibility to up-sell or down-sell clients, ensuring you don't leave any money on the table.

By offering a high-ticket offer or service on a payment plan, you can reach your monthly revenue targets faster. While your high-ticket offer is not scalable, your one-to-many and group offers are. This means you can serve more clients simultaneously and maximise your impact and social proof. 'It's essential to recognise that not everyone will afford or want your highest ticket offer, and similarly, some may prefer the close proximity that your high-ticket offering provides over the broader access of group programmes.

In the early stages of your business, you may not have the audience size or engagement necessary to generate the sales volume required for your low- and mid-ticket offers. By strategically selling both high-ticket and group offers, you can effectively grow your client base while giving yourself the chance to establish a solid foundation for your business.

THE IMPORTANCE OF SCALABILITY IN YOUR BUSINESS

Scalability is a vital element to consider as part of your business model. Without it, you'll find yourself constantly exchanging your time for money — a scenario that's far from ideal if you value freedom like I do. Scalability comes from implementing one-to-many offers, creating a complementary profitable product suite, encouraging client retention and building a solid reputation, authority and awareness around you, your work and your brand.

To truly embrace scalability in your business, there are several strategies to consider. The first one often gets overlooked: focusing on the ROI from your existing audience and clients. These people are already your hottest leads and buyers. This makes them your best opportunity for growth because they've already engaged in your services.

Too many entrepreneurs fixate solely on building new audiences and attracting new clients, which is, of course, essential for growth. However, this focus often causes them to overlook the low-hanging fruit — the clients who are already in their ecosystem.

When you aim to elevate the scalability of your business, prioritise high client retention levels. Nurturing your existing clients is not only easier than constantly chasing new ones, but it costs you less in time and money.

In addition to focusing on your existing audience, there are other crucial strategies to enhance scalability in your business. One of the most obvious is to provide the best client experience and ROI for your current clients. This is a fundamental principle of Business 101: as business owners and entrepreneurs, our clients should always be our top priority. Supporting your clients with exactly what they need at each stage of their journey is essential. By doing this, you not only create an exceptional experience for them but also foster loyalty and retention. When clients feel valued and well-supported, they are much more likely to stay with you for the long haul.

Example of a Clear Client Pathway with a Profitable Product Suite

Let's take a look at how a well-structured, profitable product suite can elevate your client lifetime value using the strategies 'we've discussed.

Imagine your new client, Anne. She starts by purchasing your group program for £2,000. After completing the group program, Anne is so impressed with the experience and the results she's achieved that she decides to join your mastermind for £12,000.

During her time in the mastermind, Anne thrives and experiences big results. This motivates her to take the next step: enrolling in your one-to-one mentoring programme at £34,000. After completing the mentoring, Anne is keen to continue her journey and growth and chooses to join your higher-level mastermind for an additional £24,000.

In this scenario, instead of limiting Anne's client lifetime value to just £2,000 by offering only a mid-ticket group programme, 'you've strategically included higher-ticket options in your product suite. By making these offers the obvious next step in her journey, you've successfully elevated Anne's client lifetime value to an impressive £72,000, instead of limiting it to just £2,000.

This example demonstrates the power of creating a clear client pathway that guides clients seamlessly from one offer to the next, maximising both their transformation and your business revenue.

MASTERING YOUR PRICING AND PACKAGING

I often get asked by clients and people in my audience, *"Tania, what should I price my offer at?"*. Unfortunately, there is no black-or-white answer. However, there are some clear guidelines that I can give you to help support you when it comes to pricing your offers, including your high-ticket offers within your business model.

When it comes to pricing your offers, several key factors come into play. First, consider the value of the transformation that your offer delivers; the greater the transformation, the higher the price point should be. Next, evaluate how much of your time will be required to deliver the offer — more time invested should correspond to a higher price. Additionally, think about the level of close proximity your clients will have to you and your team within each offer; the more access they receive, the higher the price point can be. Lastly, assess the resources and support included with your offer, as these elements will also inform your pricing decisions. By thoughtfully considering these aspects, you can effectively set prices that genuinely reflect the value of your offers.

One common misconception about pricing offers is that entrepreneurs often base their prices solely on the time spent in delivery and the specific resources included. This approach typically results in underpricing, leaving the entrepreneur feeling undervalued. Instead, especially for high-ticket offers, pricing should reflect several key factors: your level of expertise, the magnitude of the expected results and the speed and ease at which those results can be achieved. Additionally, consider the reduced risk that clients experience — what I refer to as the four expert values (as discussed in Chapter Three). By focusing on these elements, you can set prices that accurately represent the value you provide.

Your clients aren't purely investing in the time they get with you, they are investing in your knowledge, your experience, your leadership and the investments which you have made in your self-development and business.

Another strong piece of advice I want to give you is to avoid pricing yourself in comparison with entrepreneurs who are ten steps ahead of you. Doing this won't serve you or your conversions. Remember, you are not pricing based on your competition. Yes, it's important to know what your competition is offering and what their price points are, but if the value, support and expected results from your offers far exceed your competition, you do not need to price the same.

Since this book dives deeply into high-ticket sales, it's essential for me to provide you with specific pricing tips tailored to your high-ticket offers. First and foremost, be cautious about ever discounting your high-ticket offers. Rather than applying discounts, consider offering alternative incentives to encourage people to invest in your offers or services. Discounts can devalue your high-ticket, high-proximity work, so I advise avoiding them for these particular offers.

Once you set your price, you need to wholeheartedly, energetically back it with conviction. Remember, this means you need to go first. You won't ever have high-ticket clients unless you make the one decision to create, launch and sell a high-ticket offer at a high-ticket price point. So, commit to going first and energetically backing your price points once you have sent them. What I've seen happen in the past is when people charge too low for their close proximity, higher ticket offers. This can often lead to resentment. We don't want this.

Price wisely and remember that your pricing can always go up. What pricing too low also does is reduce the perceived value of your offer in your audience's mind, which discourages them from investing. However, at the other end of the spectrum, charge too high at a price where you don't feel comfortable, and you will make no sales because this will be obvious and palpable to your audience.

Finally, establishing a clear pricing structure for each level of offer in your product suite is important. This means you should distinctly differentiate each offer by its price, support, value and expected results. If your low-, mid-, and high-ticket offers are too similar in these aspects, it can confuse potential clients and negatively impact their buying decision. By clearly defining what each offer entails, you'll make it easier for clients to understand the unique benefits of each option and encourage them to choose the right fit for their needs.

To conclude Chapter Seven, remember to create a product suite that feels like a home for your clients. Do this and they will stay forever. It's your job to ensure you can offer support to your clients at every stage of their journey and every level of their financial accessibility. This means elevated reputation, client retention, referrals and revenue for your business while also co-creating the most incredible results with your clients.

ACCESS YOUR EXCLUSIVE HIGH-TICKET MASTERY MINI-COURSE

Simply go to **bit.ly/Highticketmethodbookcourse** to access your Chapter Seven resources which will help you with building out your profitable product suite.

EIGHT
PERSONALISED EXPERIENCES PAY

THE PSYCHOLOGY OF PERSONALISATION

Sustainable success in business, especially in the high-ticket, premium sector, is all about how you make your clients feel. The emotions you evoke in your clients are what they'll always remember, more than the price.

Personalised experiences activate powerful psychological principles that, when executed effectively, significantly influence how clients perceive and engage with your services. Personalisation directly impacts the buying process, and the level of investment clients are willing to make. Generally speaking, the more personalised the experience, the higher the price point you can command.

Personalised experiences elevate your client's sense of excitement and engagement because a bespoke experience will resonate more with their individual preferences, needs and desires. Client satisfaction soars when they are met with more personalisation, which, in turn, creates a unique and more meaningful connection between you and your client. By applying the psychology-backed principles which I'll be covering in this chapter, you will create experiences for your clients which resonate deeply with them, foster loyalty and set the foundations for long-lasting relationships between you and your clients.

When it comes to the personalised experiences you deliver for your clients, your job is to unlock and implement my science-backed, high-ticket approach to design and seamlessly deliver the ultimate, premium, high-ticket experience for your clients.

In this chapter, I'll guide you through the process of transforming your clients into 'forever clients' — those who consistently choose to benefit from your expertise and support. In turn, they will generate consistent, recurring income for your business while elevating client retention rates and bringing valuable high-ticket referrals to your business.

You know the feeling of treating yourself to something special — a Louis Vuitton bag, Hermès sandals, a stunning necklace or a beautiful evening dress. Purchases like these elevate your sense of achievement and often (but not always), lead you to care for these items more than your everyday buys. When you invest in something valuable and extraordinary, the experience becomes memorable and impactful.

Consider the difference between stepping into a luxury car showroom like BMW or Mercedes compared to a second-hand car garage. The level of personalisation in a new car showroom is amplified; every detail is designed to create an exceptional experience that makes you feel valued as a customer. Sales executives in these premium environments are trained to go the extra mile, recognising that their efforts lead to premium customers, higher sales and increased commissions. They understand that cultivating long-term loyalty by embracing the power of personalisation is crucial to elevating their client lifetime value.

Which sales environment would you prefer? For me, it's the new car showroom every time, simply because of the elevated personalisation and more enjoyable experience overall.

As an expert delivering a service, integrating strategies to enhance the level of personalisation you deliver for your clients isn't a 'nice-to-have' for your business, it's a strategic 'must-have' for sustained success in a competitive and noisy industry like the online space.

Personalised experiences tap into the power of exclusivity psychology. Think about a time when you really wanted something luxurious or unique. That exciting and possibly slightly nerve-wracking feeling of being special, like a VIP, stems from the power of the degree of personalisation delivered during the buying process and exclusivity. When you purchase something where the principles of personalisation are applied to the buying process, it makes you feel unique and makes the experience feel extraordinary.

This is exactly the emotion you want to evoke in your premium clients. People want to feel special and to enjoy personalised experiences that not everyone can enjoy. By leveraging personalisation and exclusivity psychology, you create an atmosphere where your clients feel valued and unique — exactly how they should feel when engaging with your premium offers and services.

WHY DO HIGH-TICKET CLIENTS WANT PERSONALISATION?

Personalisation evokes a multitude of psychological reactions, making it a key element of the high-ticket client attraction, sales and conversion process. Personalisation enhances your client's sense of individuality and identity. It makes them feel special, just like the Mercedes new car showroom sales executive would.

Have you ever experienced a salesperson complimenting you on how nice you look, admiring your watch or noting how cute your children are? These small gestures of personalisation significantly enhance the overall buying experience, making it feel more meaningful and relevant to you as an individual. This approach is particularly important when working with high-ticket clients. By acknowledging their individuality and tailoring your interactions, you position yourself as the expert they can trust to help them resolve their specific issues and achieve their goals.

A personalised experience fosters a greater sense of motivation and engagement in your clients to make the most of their investment with you, largely because they are receiving a bespoke service relative to their needs and goals.

By default, higher levels of personalisation in the experiences you deliver create more emotional connection between you and your clients, because you will get to know more and more about them, their lives, their businesses and so on... just like the Mercedes car sales executive who will know all about you, your kids, where you live and other personal elements of your life. As a result, the level of control your clients feel is greater, as they are receiving a service specifically created with them in mind, which, in turn, fosters a greater sense of control and autonomy over the journey on which they are working with you.

As already mentioned, the level of perceived value your clients hold relative to your offer, as a result of the level of personalisation you provide them, is greater, making them prepared to pay more. Lastly, there is a strong correlation between the level of bespoke personalised support received and the likelihood and speed at which your clients expect to achieve their desired goals.

Understanding these psychological drivers empowers you to intentionally incorporate personalisation into your offers and services. By acknowledging and leveraging these factors, you are equipped to create experiences that not only meet the needs of your clients but also resonate on a deeper psychological level with your clients, therefore enhancing the overall experience and levels of satisfaction your clients have, which directly impacts your client retention.

Consider your own experiences for a moment. You would likely be willing to pay a premium price for a bag, phone case or clothing for your children if they were personalised with your name or your children's names on them. This principle applies directly to personalising your offers for high-ticket clients. When you create personalised experiences, your ideal, high-ticket clients will be more inclined to invest at a higher price point.

DATA-DRIVEN PERSONALISATION

With the technology available to us today, it's so easy to unlock the power of personalisation and take it to the next level by strategically leveraging the unlimited data you can now collect on your clients during their experiences and journeys with you.

Data-driven personalisation involves using data collection and insights from your clients to tailor your services, approaches and content, making them truly bespoke and personalised for them. The simplest way to explain this is by thinking of a personal trainer and how they work with their clients in current times. They'll get their clients to track their weight, diet, exercise and even sleep, amongst other physiological trackers, using apps so they can implement data-driven personalisation in their work for better client results. You can do this, too, by using the apps, resources, surveys, questionnaires etc. relevant to the work that you do.

Examples of the tools you can use to deliver a truly bespoke and personalised experience for your clients include survey and questionnaire tools such as Google Forms, Typeform and

Survey Monkey. You can use these tools to collect information on your client's goals, preferences, feedback and expectations before, during and even after their experience of working with you, to continuously inform the work you do with your clients.

Client on-boarding forms are a vital part of how I run my online business. They enable me to collect comprehensive data on where my clients are in business, their challenges, their goals and what specifically they need my support with to achieve their end goals. These forms serve as the baseline for tailoring my approach with my high-ticket clients. We currently use Typeform for this.

Feedback processes are essential to ensure your clients receive the support and achieve the progress they want. To do this, consider scheduling regular feedback sessions with your clients where they can openly share their thoughts, feelings and expectations about their experience so far. This doesn't have to be in person. As an example, in my Wealthy Mastermind, my clients are expected to fill out their weekly progress forms every Friday, which give my team and me powerful information and personalised data on their wins, their challenges, what support they feel they benefit from and what further support they may want from us. This feedback is then read by my team and me to ensure we act on anything mentioned which is relevant to my clients and their progress, to enhance their progress and experience.

Goal-tracking resources are powerful tools to identify and measure progress against the goals your clients want to achieve. I highly encourage you to implement regular trackers in your business to keep on top of your client's actions and progress. For example, in my Wealthy Mastermind, we currently use a bespoke PDF form for my clients, which identifies their weekly sales and revenue goals and the relevant actions they need to take to achieve them. It also allows them to review their weekly progress and action-taking for any improvements needed.

These are just a few examples of the types of resources and tools you can implement in your business to gather data and implement data-driven personalisation into your client work and experiences' It's essential to emphasise though that any data-driven tools, resources, and collected data must be utilised in accordance with ethical standards, privacy regulations, security protocols and data protection guidelines specific to your country and region, to protect both your clients and your business.

THE PSYCHOLOGY OF HIGH-TICKET CLIENT EXPERIENCE AND EXPECTATIONS

It goes without saying that with a higher price tag comes higher expectations. High-ticket clients have greater expectations than other client types. Your power, as the go-to expert in your niche for high-ticket clients, is in understanding the expectations which your ideal, high-ticket clients have in the first place. Understanding these expectations is the first step to exceeding them, which is your aim as a high-ticket expert and one who creates and delivers high-ticket experiences. In this section, I will outline what high-ticket buyers expect when they decide to hire you and give you the necessary insights on how you can go above and beyond these expectations.

The first two expectations are fundamental and serve as key lessons in Business 101, so it's essential to address them upfront:

The first expectation is that high-ticket clients expect industry-leading knowledge and expertise from you as their chosen expert. This means you must master your craft and your unique genius. Avoid selling or delivering offers and experiences related to topics that you haven't fully mastered; instead, focus on mastery and leadership in your niche. You don't need to be an expert in every area of your industry, but you should be a master in your specific zone of genius.

The second expectation centres on confidentiality and privacy. It's essential to emphasise your commitment to maintaining confidentiality right from the beginning of every working relationship. During the on-boarding process, make it clear that working with you creates a safe space for open and honest dialogue. This reassurance not only fosters trust but also encourages a more impactful collaboration. Importantly, these expectations apply to all clients, not just those who invest in high-ticket offerings.

Your high-ticket clients will expect to achieve progress and results as they move towards their goals by working with you. Ensure you discuss exactly where your client is and what they want to achieve from the outset so you can track their progress, ideally before they become a paying client.

To ensure this happens, it's your job to implement regular progress assessments and collect performance metrics to track and demonstrate their ROI from working with you. As a side note (but a relevant one), a key strategy which I implement early on with my clients is focusing on them getting results fast and early on. This triggers high satisfaction levels and dopamine releases which elevate their client satisfaction levels. They then start to make an association between their wins and achievements and working with you, and their sense of excitement and motivation to continue remains or elevates. The longer it takes for clients to get results, the more likely it is to see a drop in their satisfaction, excitement and motivation levels and you risk them disengaging.

High-ticket clients expect personalised and customised service and attention. This is why it's so important to provide a detailed on-boarding process at the start of your working relationship to understand their specific needs. This includes demonstrating flexibility in your services and delivery where possible, such as booking call times that suit both of you and finding the best-suited communication channel for you both.

Another key part of delivering a personalised experience is fast and responsive communication from you. Your high-ticket clients don't want to be waiting days for a response from you (trust me, I've been there, and you feel like you're not getting the service you expected, which can lead to you wishing you'd invested elsewhere). This is where boundary and expectation setting are important. Have clear and set expectations in your contracts as to the timeframes by which clients can expect responses from you in the worst-case scenario. For example, my close proximity and high-ticket client contracts set clear expectations that the longest they will ever wait for a response from me is forty-eight working hours. Whilst I respond almost always within the first day of receipt, usually within a few hours, it's still important to have these clear boundaries and expectations set to protect you, your business and your clients. My close proximity clients also rarely contact me on the weekends, as I have set clear expectations from the beginning of our working journey as to when they have access to me. Even if they do message me on a weekend, which is rare, they always make it clear that they don't expect a response from me by using phrases like, *"I don't expect you to get back to me over the weekend"*, because they understand the boundaries and expectations that we set from the outset.

Expectation setting for your working relationship needs to come from you first as the expert, once you've identified what the client wants, to ensure that:

- The working relationship fits your chosen business model; and
- Your client's expectations and desires are met when it comes to their progress and achieving their goals.

Your high-ticket clients will expect exclusive access to certain things as part of their premium service, so, it's important at the start of your working relationship to identify exactly what your clients get access to, what they would like access to and if it is included. Of course, we'll talk about how to 'surprise and delight' your clients throughout your working relationship, to elevate their feelings of being appreciated and their satisfaction levels. For example, I will often surprise my high-ticket clients with bonus access to extra resources or events, which they weren't previously expecting, and these 'surprise and delight' strategies go a long way. We'll cover how you can do this later in this chapter.

DESIGNING THE ULTIMATE PERSONALISED PREMIUM EXPERIENCE

When it comes to designing and delivering a personalised premium experience, a client-centric approach means not only do you meet and exceed your client expectations, but you also build a loyal client base and elevate your client retention as a result. I advise my clients to create a journey map for each of their high-ticket clients. A simple breakdown of a personalised client journey map, and the stages at which you can add extra levels of personalisation for your clients is shown below.

PERSONALISED CLIENT JOURNEY MAP

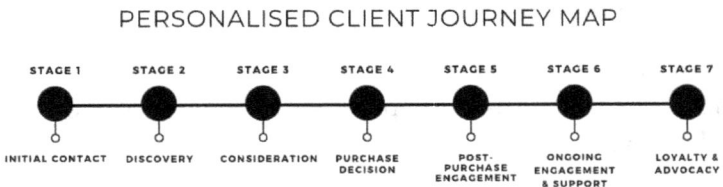

STAGE 1	STAGE 2	STAGE 3	STAGE 4	STAGE 5	STAGE 6	STAGE 7
INITIAL CONTACT	DISCOVERY	CONSIDERATION	PURCHASE DECISION	POST-PURCHASE ENGAGEMENT	ONGOING ENGAGEMENT & SUPPORT	LOYALTY & ADVOCACY

Crafting a truly transformational client experience doesn't require perfection at every stage; rather, it is based on thoughtfully integrating elements that resonate with your high-ticket clients. This involves personalising your interactions with your clients, offering exclusive content to highlight their status as VIP clients and ensuring that the value they receive far exceeds their investment in your services. Additionally, aim for seamless delivery wherever possible, clearly set expectations and boundaries and provide a defined client pathway. This pathway should guide clients on which resources to access, what to implement and when, ensuring they feel supported and held throughout the process. By consistently applying these principles, you create a memorable and enjoyable client experience that fosters exceptional results, long-term relationships and loyal clients for your business.

We're now going to cover the exact steps you need to create and deliver a positive and memorable personalised premium experience for your clients, to ensure that the experience is seamless for your clients.

THOROUGH ON-BOARDING AND OFF-BOARDING PROCESSES WITH CLEAR TIMELINES

You'll start your client relationship with a thorough client on-boarding process and equally, when it comes to the end of your working relationship, you'll end with a solid off-boarding process too. On-boarding needs to include in-depth discussions about where your client is in life or business, their struggles, what they want to achieve and what support they want from you, setting preferences for training types and communication, expectations and boundaries. By having these concrete processes in place, you can get a clear understanding from the start of the exact support they need, and it allows you to tailor your approach accordingly.

When off-boarding, it's equally essential to create a memorable experience for your client. Start by reviewing and celebrating how far they've come to acknowledge the growth and progress they've achieved. A one-on-one meeting, call or a personalised moment to wrap up the journey is a great way to reflect on their accomplishments and discuss next steps. Gathering feedback during this phase is invaluable for refining your service.

While feedback should be consistently sought and acted upon throughout the relationship, this final stage offers a chance for constructive and comprehensive reflection. Extend an invitation to continue working together by offering the next logical step in your service, ensuring they know exactly how they can continue benefiting from your expertise. A thoughtful gift is a nice final touch, adding an unexpected surprise for your client to show your appreciation and reinforce their experience with you.

Regular Client Check-Ins and Expectation Assessments

This refers to scheduling regular check-ins to assess and reassess your client's progress and expectations throughout their journey. As your client's needs evolve, staying informed helps you adjust your approach and set the stage for further growth and clear expectations.

Clear Communication

The more you foster safe, open and transparent communication channels from the beginning, the more expansion your client can create by working with you. This builds trust and allows your clients to raise any concerns or struggles so you can address any concerns or make any adjustments necessary and proactively.

Over Deliver on Value

Your job as the expert is to consistently exceed expectations by consistently providing more value (and extra, unexpected value) than promised. Your job is to go above and beyond, not in a way which leads you to burnout, but in a way which leads to your high-ticket clients feeling appreciated, heard and fully supported. This can look like surprising your clients with unexpected gifts such as welcome gifts, experiences, additional resources, exclusive invitations, insights or support, which all reinforce the perception of a premium and personalised service.

Personalised Feedback and Recognition

This requires you to provide continuous feedback, recognition and celebrations tailored to your client's progress, achievements and challenges. Acknowledging and celebrating your client milestones in a personalised and thoughtful way will strengthen your client-expert relationship and will enhance the overall experience for your client and you, making business feel fulfilling, fun and exciting.

YOUR ACTION PLAN FOR CREATING AND DELIVERING YOUR NEXT ULTIMATE PERSONALISED EXPERIENCE

Now, let's delve into your action plan for enhancing the overall client experience you create and deliver.

Address Your Client Pain Points Early On

Begin by anticipating and addressing your ideal client's pain points. This proactive approach involves identifying potential challenges they may face, positioning yourself as their go-to expert and shaping your action plan accordingly. By addressing these issues at the start of your working relationship, you demonstrate foresight and a commitment to ensuring a smooth and positive experience for your clients. This not only showcases your ability to manage the client journey effectively but also instils greater confidence and certainty in your clients, reinforcing your role as their trusted expert.

Create Memorable Experiences

The next key element I want you to integrate into your overall client experience and personalisation is to focus on creating memorable experiences in your working relationship. This requires some forward thinking, planning and designing with intention to create some peak memorable moments during your client journey. For example, in my current business model, all of my Wealthy Mastermind clients get bonus access to our ultimate luxury retreat. As this is already included in the experience that they are investing in with me, it is seen as a bonus. I always plan to deliver the most impactful and memorable, experience possible when my clients are on retreat with me. Memorable experiences at key points in your client journey help to create and leave lasting positive impressions which contribute to overall satisfaction levels and client loyalty.

Create Memorable Peak Moments

Now is the perfect time to introduce the Peak-End Rule (*Kahneman, D., & Tversky, A. (1999)*. *Prospect Theory: An Analysis of Decision under Risk)*, first introduced by psychologist Daniel Kahneman where they discuss the principles of human judgment and decision-making. This rule explains that people tend to remember their experiences based on the most intense moments and how those experiences conclude. In simple terms, this means you should focus on making key moments in your clients' journeys both memorable and positive.

This principle applies even to potentially challenging situations, such as handling complaints or constructive feedback. Clients are less likely to dwell on the negative aspects of these encounters; instead, they will easily recall how you managed them. So, if you find yourself facing a challenging situation, such as a client complaint or receiving constructive feedback (and you likely will as your business grows), view it as an opportunity to enhance your services or delivery. By focusing on how you resolve these situations in a memorable and positive way, you can turn challenges into powerful moments that reinforce your clients' loyalty and satisfaction.

Equally important is the need to conclude each session, programme or working relationship on a high note, maintaining your connection and leaving a lasting and positive impression.

Remember, creating and delivering personalised experiences isn't just about the overall journey; it's important to focus on both the peaks and the endings.

Now it's your turn to reflect on how you can apply Kahneman's Peak-End Rule in your business to enhance your high-ticket client personalisation and experience. How can you implement this principle to create memorable peaks and meaningful conclusions for your clients?

Surprise and Delight Gestures

If you're anything like me, you will love a surprise or an unexpected, personalised gift or gesture sent in the post. Your high-ticket clients are no different. Imagine you've just invested multi figures in your next expert or mentor and they send you a welcome gift in the post, full of lots of lovely things you weren't expecting. It makes you feel special and appreciated and that you're not just another number inside your expert's stripe account. If you're anything like me and enjoy sending gifts and surprises to others, you'll resonate with this too.

Thoughtful and personalised surprises such as sending welcome gifts, off-boarding gifts, a personalised resource, a handwritten note or exclusive VIP invitations create another level of emotional connection between your client and you and help to strengthen and enhance the overall client experience and level of personalisation which you deliver. So, have fun with this one and think of the special, exclusive ways in which you can 'surprise and delight' your premium paying clients, so you elevate their overall personalised experience and enhance the level of personalisation within the working relationship.

Adopt a Flexible and Adaptive Approach

Flexibility goes a long way in business, especially when you are paid high prices. By being flexible with times, meeting locations, resources access et cetera, you can demonstrate your commitment to your clients' success, their personal needs and requirements and it ensures that your services remain relevant and impactful to each client, which will only further elevate the results you co-create with your clients.

Solicit and Act on Feedback

It goes without saying that when delivering any experience, particularly at the higher-end level, you continue to actively seek feedback from your clients and use it to make continuous improvements. There is no other way to actively improve your services in a way that is meaningful to your clients and at the high-ticket level, it is expected. Equally, there is no sense in actively seeking feedback and then not acting on it where relevant, so make sure that when asking for feedback, you act on it and communicate how changes are being made to your clients. By doing this, you show your clients a level of commitment to improving your services and overall client experience, which is based on how your client feels and their input. It ultimately fosters a collaborative and responsive experience which further enhances your entire client journey.

THE PRICE I WAS PREPARED TO PAY

Here's a personal example of my own that clearly demonstrates the power of personalisation when attracting high-ticket buyers. For the last few years, I'd had my eye on owning a Louis Vuitton 'Neverfull' handbag. I'd wanted one for years. I had the opportunity to buy it in London, but I always stopped myself, knowing I had a retreat planned in Beverly Hills and I wanted the purchase to feel special, because I'd never invested in a luxury bag at this price before.

Because I knew I was going to be in Beverly Hills for that retreat, I decided that instead of buying the handbag I wanted in London, I would buy the handbag at the Louis Vuitton store on Rodeo Drive, one of the most luxurious shopping streets in the world, as a treat and to celebrate the things I'd achieved that year. When I stepped into the store, I was met with an atmosphere that made me feel special, almost like a VIP. The salespeople greeted me with warmth, offering champagne as they presented my friends and me with a selection of items to try on. The entire experience was personalised, with every detail meticulously crafted to make me feel valued.

When I finally bought the handbag, I realised I was paying a premium simply for the experience of buying it in such an iconic location. Did that bother me? Not at all! The chance to buy a luxury handbag from the Louis Vuitton store on Rodeo Drive was a once-in-a-lifetime opportunity and it felt worth every dollar (I actually don't have shopping sprees like this often at all, contrary to what some might think. Spending money on 'things' is still something I can't always justify. This is part of my relationship with money that I still need to work on). This experience is a great example of the power of personalisation; just like high-ticket clients, I was willing to invest more for a unique experience that resonated with my desires and aspirations and ultimately, which was personalised. Whilst I don't do things like that often, it was an experience that I'll never forget.

By putting all of the actions I've given you in this chapter into place when designing and delivering your personalised experiences, you give yourself and your business every opportunity to create a seamless experience for your clients, which, in turn, enables them to enjoy it more and become loyal, raving customers and fans of yours and your brand.

ACCESS YOUR EXCLUSIVE HIGH-TICKET MASTERY MINI-COURSE

Head to **bit.ly/Highticketmethodbookcourse** to access your Chapter Eight resources to take the experiences that you deliver to the next level.

NINE
BUILD A STRONG REPUTATION AS THE EXPERT WHO GETS RESULTS

"BUILD THE REPUTATION AS THE EXPERT WHO GETS PROVEN RESULTS AND YOU'LL NEVER HAVE A PROBLEM WITH MAKING SALES."

— TANIA KING-MOHAMMAD

You've watched others in your industry get recognition and build reputations for delivering outstanding results and now, you want to build the same stage for yourself. You understand how powerful this can be for your reputation, sales, referrals, and ultimately the growth of your business. This is exactly what we are covering in Chapter Nine.

Prioritising your clients' results and return on investment (ROI) is not just good business; it's the foundation of building your business and multiplying your impact and income. When you consistently deliver exceptional value and elevate your client outcomes, you create a powerful ripple effect of success for both your clients and your business. Satisfied clients become loyal advocates for your brand and refer others to your services, which helps your legacy of impact to grow exponentially as you establish yourself as the expert who delivers proven results.

However, achieving this reputation requires more than just knowledge. This, of course, is rooted in mastery of your zone of genius and the strategies you teach. It's essential to ensure that your clients' successes aren't just one-off, short-lived experiences which aren't repeatable because burnout becomes an issue for your clients. You build the reputation of the expert who gets proven results by combining mastery of your zone of genius with a client-centric approach, focusing on raising and maintaining your client's sense of positivity and well-being. This holistic focus not only fosters long-lasting results for your clients but also solidifies your status as a trusted authority in your field because by focusing on your client's well-being alongside the strategies you use, you promote longer-term, sustainable client success.

This is where my background as a Positive Psychology Coach comes into my work. Positive Psychology, founded by Professor Martin Seligman, is defined as *"the study of strengths and virtues that enable individuals, communities and organisations to thrive"*. (*Gable and Haidt, (2005) Sheldon and King (2001)*. It's often referred to as 'the science of positivity', 'the science of well-being' and 'the science of human potential'. By leveraging the principles of both business strategy and the science of positivity in my work, I'm able to create a synergistic effect with my work which amplifies my client results and potential. Importantly, it's a fundamental pillar to client success which lots of business owners are missing.

ADOPTING A CLIENT-CENTRIC APPROACH

One of the biggest mistakes I see many entrepreneurs make, which significantly impacts their sales and client results, is their lack of a 360-degree client-centric approach when it comes to supporting their clients. Many business owners are so blinkered by pushing their one, specific strategy onto their clients that they forget there is a unique individual on the other side and that one 'cookie cutter' or 'one-size-fits-all' approach just won't apply to all of their ideal clients, even if they fit their umbrella ideal client criteria. This is their downfall for their client impact and results, and ultimately their business revenue.

To create the biggest impact and results with your clients, using a holistic, 360-degree approach is your key to fast-track their desired success and results, and, as a by-product, your success.

This means not just focusing on the results they want to create. You also have to take into consideration how that individual client operates, what gets them into flow and the strategies, activities and people with which they thrive. Therefore, when it comes to the strategies you use, maintaining your client's sense of well-being and positivity should be at the heart of all you do. After all, your clients can have every strategy in the world nailed, but if they don't have the tools and resources in place to maintain a high sense of well-being and positivity to keep implementing those strategies, burnout is inevitable, and their results will be short-lived and unsustainable.

You're ready to become known as the expert who gets proven results, so I'm going to highlight some tools and principles that will help you do exactly this. Achieve this, and you'll never be short of leads and high-ticket clients waiting to hire you for your expertise, whatever your price point.

Your clients' sense of well-being is directly linked to their success. By incorporating key principles from the science of positivity and well-being into your work, you can focus on their strengths and what is already positive about themselves and their actions. This approach allows you to support your clients in nurturing their zone of genius, fostering a growth mindset and maintaining a solution-focused perspective, all of which directly impact their decision-making, progress, consistency and overall results. Ultimately, you empower them to achieve their desired outcomes while experiencing greater happiness and fulfillment, rather than struggling with feelings of despair, overwhelm and burnout.

These key principles are crucial for creating transformational results and delivering elevated ROI for your clients, which, in turn, enhances your reputation and increases your revenue. I have much more to share about my **Elevate: The Results Elevator System** and my seven-step Results Elevate System. This framework equips my clients to combine the power of positivity and well-being science with their unique strategies to enhance their clients' well-being and results, ultimately elevating their reputations. Exploring this in depth goes beyond the scope of this book but I'll teach you the key principles here.

HARNESSING THE SCIENCE OF POSITIVITY FOR TRANSFORMATIONAL CLIENT RESULTS

Using key principles rooted in the science of positivity, you can establish yourself as the expert known for getting your clients results in several ways. At the forefront of the science of positive psychology is the focus on identifying and leveraging an individual's strengths. By helping your clients identify and embrace their unique strengths to achieve their goals, rather than concentrating on perceived weaknesses, you can create bespoke, personalised experiences and strategies. This ensures that your approach is tailored to each individual, moving away from a one-size-fits-all mentality.

Success in life and business relies strongly on an individual's resilience to keep going during challenging times. Resilience building is another key element of the science of positive psychology and empowering your clients with resilience skills and strategies by connecting them to their 'why' reason – why they do what they do, their meaning and their purpose is a fundamental piece when it comes to elevating and maintaining your clients' sense of positivity, well-being and potential. You will see that as your clients continue to overcome challenges with your support, they will start to associate working with you and your help with how they bounce back and thrive through challenges.

Success in life and business doesn't happen by chance. The same is true for your clients. To achieve their goals, clear targets must be established, accompanied by a well-defined action plan aligned to them and their strengths. A cornerstone of the science of positivity is the emphasis on setting and achieving meaningful SMART goals (goals which are specific, measurable, achievable, relevant and time-bound). By integrating this approach into your work, you can effectively support your clients on their journey toward success. As they accomplish their goals, they will recognise your expertise and guidance as a catalyst for their growth and achievements, leading them to associate part of their results with your support and expertise.

In addition to setting meaningful goals, it's crucial to measure and track your clients' progress. This not only provides you with valuable baseline and progress information but also allows your clients to witness quantifiable improvements in their lives or businesses. Creating this awareness of their progress fuels their motivation and momentum, encouraging them to continue progressing toward their goals. As they do, they will increasingly attribute part of their achievements to your expertise and support.

A key principle of the science of well-being and positivity is to always look for solutions in every situation. The more you can support your clients in looking for and implementing a solution-oriented approach, by supporting them in developing a growth mindset, you position yourself as the expert who helps their clients achieve tangible and lasting results.

Business and life can often be challenging and, as entrepreneurs, we often find ourselves questioning why we started our businesses, especially when faced with the curve balls that life throws our way. I sometimes joke with my clients, audience and even my husband that I would rather pack everything in and head to the nearest clothing store to take a job as a sales assistant on the shop floor. Honestly, the temptation to do this comes up quite frequently. I imagine that working on the shop floor would feel less stressful, more light-hearted, and, quite frankly, more fun at times. Running a business can be testing and stressful, making it easy for negative emotions to creep in and impact how we feel and operate. Recognising this challenge for your clients is the first step toward helping them find balance and joy in their entrepreneurial journey.

The reason I mention my shopworker example (which my clients have heard often), is that it's easy to forget to bring positive emotions and uplifting experiences into our work when we're so focused on running our businesses instead of working on them. This is where the science of well-being plays a crucial role: we must consciously cultivate positive emotions in our interactions with our clients. The more you elevate your clients' sense of positivity, the more they will experience increased gratitude, happiness and fulfilment... and associate these positive changes with your support and expertise.

Think about how you can evoke more positive emotions in your clients through your work together. It could be as simple as sending surprise gifts or reminding them of how incredible they are at what they do. Even a straightforward acknowledgement of their worth as human beings can make a significant impact. It doesn't take much, but it's essential to recognise the power of fostering positive emotions. Doing so not only enhances your clients' well-being and productivity but ultimately leads to better and longer-term results.

Focusing on a holistic approach with your clients by combining your unique strategies with a focus on elevating and maintaining their levels of well-being and positivity, will ultimately empower and enable your clients to achieve long-term impact and success because they have the tools and resources to achieve long-term results and avoid burnout. This also means that your expertise and support become associated with the positive longer-lasting results your clients are achieving and, ultimately, a reputation of the expert known for getting results with high-ticket clients.

By leveraging the principles of both business strategy and positive psychology in my business, clients are not only able to achieve their goals more effectively, but they are also able to unlock new levels of long-term growth, fulfilment and success, instead of results which are short-lived and not repeatable. Long-term, sustainable results for your clients means your reputation grows as the expert known for getting results, which is magnetic when it comes to attracting more of the high-ticket clients you want. This is why *The High-Ticket Method*® has an entire pillar dedicated to this powerful holistic approach.

BUILDING LOYAL CLIENT ADVOCATES: THE CLIENTS-AND-CASH-ON-REPEAT SYSTEM

You now know exactly what you need to do to stand out from the crowd and support your clients in achieving the most incredible results, whilst at the same time elevating your reputation as the expert known for getting results. By harnessing the science of positivity and bringing it into your work, you get to transform your client outcomes and ROI, which leads to elevated levels of client satisfaction, loyalty and advocacy for you and your brand. This ultimately ends up in your clients indirectly selling your offers for you. Believe me, there is no better sales strategy than having your clients sell for you.

The key, positivity-based principles we've discussed during this chapter are designed to enhance the strengths, resilience and positive emotions of your clients, enabling them to be better problem-solvers and achieve their goals more effectively and, usually, faster. This will elevate their overall performance and, ultimately, skyrocket their results.

Better client results directly translate into increased ROIs for your clients and, indirectly, for you and your business. This is because happier, more successful clients are more likely to continue investing in your services and are more likely to recommend your services to others. This is where my powerful **Clients-and-Cash-on-Repeat system** comes in.

THE CLIENTS-AND-CASH-ON-REPEAT SYSTEM

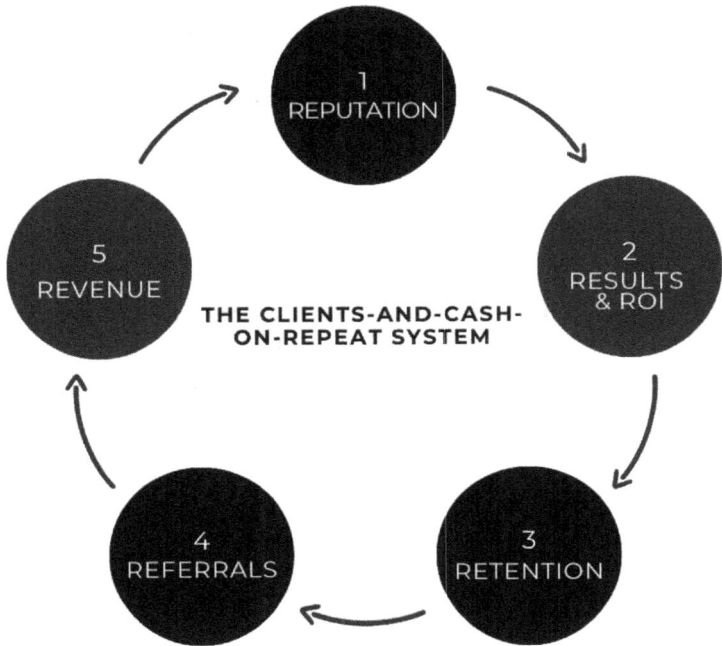

At the centre of the **Clients-and-Cash-on-Repeat system**, lies a focus on driving incredible client results and ROI. As you do this, as you now know, your reputation skyrockets as the expert known for getting clients results. Because your clients are getting incredible results through your powerful combination of both strategy and focusing on your client's sense of positivity, they start to associate their elevated results and ROI with working with you and your expertise. This leads to elevated client retention levels, i.e., more clients continuing to work with you.

Because your clients are getting such incredible results and they associate part of their achievements with working with you, they don't stop raving about how good you are at what you do and how much they have grown by working with you. They start to refer people in their network to you, which means you start to bring in high-ticket client referrals.

All of these five key powerful steps within this system directly contribute to and are correlated with your elevated revenue, because your clients are getting the most incredible, life-changing results, you've got a growing reputation, your retention levels are high, and you are receiving consistent high-ticket client referrals. It's a win-win situation for your high-ticket clients, you and your business.

Helping your clients get elevated results isn't just about achieving success once. This is the catalyst for exponential growth for your clients and your business. As happier, more successful clients continue to invest in your services and passionately and loyally advocate for your brand, the effect of your work and impact extends beyond just the work you do with them, further driving your elevated results, reputation, revenue and lasting transformation for both you and your clients.

In conclusion, the more you focus on your client results, success and ROI, by combining the power of your unique strategy and the science of positivity and well-being, the more loyal and satisfied your clients will be and, as a byproduct, the more elevated your reputation and revenue will be too. So, this is your reminder to always lead with value and service delivery and focus on a holistic, client-centric approach to your work with your clients. Not only will your clients achieve significantly better results, but you will too, as a natural by-product of your integrity-driven, ethical approach. With a strong focus on being client-centric, your success is built on delivering real value and creating real impact and change.

ACCESS YOUR EXCLUSIVE HIGH-TICKET MASTERY MINI-COURSE

Simply go to **bit.ly/Highticketmethodbookcourse** to access your Chapter Nine resources and consolidate our work further on how to build your reputation as the go-to expert for high-ticket clients who gets results.

TEN
PREMIUM SALES STRATEGIES

You're ready to become the go-to expert in your industry and to get paid much more for the work you love without multiplying your workload. You want to attract clients who don't hesitate to hire and pay you the premium rates that really excite you, far beyond what you used to charge. It's time to master premium sales strategies, which are very different from those used for low- and mid-ticket offers.

The strategies that work for selling lower-priced offers simply don't apply to high-ticket sales in the same way. Trying to use them is like hanging your laundry out to dry in the rain — it just won't work. In this chapter, I'll share the strategies you need to shift your sales mindset, boost your results and sell your high-ticket offers in a way that feels authentic, without leaving you or your potential clients feeling pressured or out of alignment with your values because you'll be applying them in a way that is both ethical and aligned with integrity.

I know my sales strategies are effective and integrity-led because many clients share that one of the key reasons they choose to work with me is the absence of them feeling pressured to buy in the buying process. I remain detached from the outcome, allowing my clients to make decisions that feel right for them, rather than feeling rushed or cornered into making a decision they are not ready for. This approach is important to me, as I only want to work with clients who recognise their readiness and take aligned action to hire me as their go-to expert.

LET'S TALK ABOUT SALES BABY

Sales and business are simple; they don't need to be complicated. People often overcomplicate them, but you don't have to. At its core, successful sales is about solving your ideal client's problem so they can achieve their desired outcome. Sales is simply a transaction — your clients see the value in your offer and commit to purchasing it in exchange for money. It's an equal exchange, not just you asking for money.

If you feel awkward or uncomfortable when it comes to selling, this chapter will help push you out of your comfort zone, but in a good way, where you operate well within your core values and with integrity. But you need to remember, you are not begging for someone to give you their money. With sales, you are promoting a fair exchange where you deliver a service, and your high-ticket clients pay for it. As you already know, I'm not here for bro-style marketing and sales tactics. This chapter will provide the mindset shifts and strategies you need so that selling becomes easy, natural and second nature for you.

IT IS YOUR JOB TO SELL CONSISTENTLY

How you feel about sales will directly impact how much revenue your business generates. Making the conscious decision to step into the elevated mindset that sales get to feel easy, simple and exciting, and combining this with selling consistently and daily is going to be the catalyst for you to multiply your revenue.

As a business owner, it's your responsibility to sell, unapologetically, every single day, and *not* just when you feel like it. Imagine walking into your local supermarket because you're running low on groceries. There's no bread, making toast an impossible option for your kids, who are complaining about wanting nothing else but *"toast, toast, toast"*. You also don't have enough milk for your morning coffee, desperately needed after a night of unwelcome, early wake-up calls from your little ones. Now, picture stepping into your local Sainsbury's, only to be told that they don't feel like selling bread today and that milk won't be available until next week when they 'feel like' offering it. This isn't how brick-and-mortar businesses operate, and, as a service-based business owner, it shouldn't be how you operate either.

When you reframe your sales approach to being service-led, focusing entirely on solving your client's problems, your sales are almost guaranteed. I see so many entrepreneurs make their marketing, messaging or content too much about them when everything we do as entrepreneurs should be solely focused on our clients. When you shift the spotlight away from yourself and onto serving your ideal high-ticket clients, the natural by-product is your sales multiplied.

Every time you post, create messaging or market, make sure it's all with a client-centric approach, always ask yourself or your team the following:

Is this relevant to my ideal client?

Why should they care about this?

How does this impact them?

By doing this and by being consistently client-centric in your approach to business, marketing and sales, the more money you'll make. So, make it less about you and all about them.

To take this a step further and connect it to your pricing (which is set to increase after reading this book), remember that business is fundamentally about solving your ideal client's problems. The greater the problem you can address, the higher the perceived value of your solution and the more you get paid. It's time to push yourself and your business beyond your comfort zone — after all, nothing exciting ever happens there. Start thinking bigger: what larger problems can you solve for your clients? By tackling these bigger challenges, you open the door to larger payouts for your business. It's time to attract the financial success you've only dreamed of until now, all through a truly client-centric approach and a clear focus on providing solutions and serving your clients.

It's time to get out of your own way when it comes to selling and to start seeing selling as the non-negotiable heartbeat of your business. Because without sales, you have no business. You have a hobby – an expensive and time-consuming one at that.

THERE IS SELLING, THEN THERE IS SELLING

There's a big difference between selling and *selling*. Many entrepreneurs struggle with negative connotations associated with sales, often influenced by the stereotypes of sleazy car salesmen and aggressive bro-marketing tactics. I understand where this comes from. If you're Generation X and from the UK like me, you probably grew up watching Del Boy from the TV programme *Only Fools and Horses* as he tried to peddle his dodgy watches and gadgets, fully aware they were often faulty or even stolen. That was hardly a lesson in selling with integrity! If you're not familiar with the show, I highly recommend checking it out; it's a classic in British comedy, but definitely don't take any sales strategies from it — your reputation and sales will probably suffer as a result!

Now, back to those car salesman stereotypes. These negative associations can be major roadblocks, preventing entrepreneurs and business owners from multiplying their sales and skyrocketing their businesses. You'll be relieved to know that this chapter won't cover any of those outdated tactics. Instead, I'll share powerful hacks and strategies designed to positively influence your ideal, high-ticket clients' buying decisions, creating a win-win for both your clients and your business. They'll benefit from your world-class, life-changing services, while you reap the rewards of being well-paid for your world-class expertise. These high-ticket sales strategies and closing techniques are rooted in ethical business practices and integrity, positioning you as the go-to expert that high-ticket clients are ready and waiting to hire and pay.

Sales Become Easier When You Do This

The fastest way to speed up your sales and make them feel easier is to identify exactly who it is that you want to speak to and communicate to only them in your content. This is identifying your ideal, premium client persona and your messaging. Remember, you want your marketing and messaging to land specifically and directly with only the ideal, high-ticket clients you want to work with. You're no longer here for a 'catch-all' marketing strategy and generic ideal client because you're scared of alienating the majority of 'potential' clients through fear of niching down too far. You're here to attract and convert the specific, high-level clients you really want to work with. The clients who are ready to pay your highest rates yet for your services, without questioning your prices or giving you the *"I can't afford it right now"* objections. You're tightening your net and only fishing for the specific catch you want, not throwing it out far and wide hoping you catch a bit of everything. This means your messaging needs to be dialled in. Remember, you're here for quality, *not* quantity.

SELL AS OFTEN AS YOU WANT TO GET PAID

Many entrepreneurs come to me feeling frustrated because they're not making the sales they want and aren't getting paid as frequently as they'd like. I teach my clients a simple yet effective formula: *the more you sell, the more you get paid.* The frequency of your sales directly correlates with your income. If you sell only once a week, you'll be lucky to get paid that often. However, if you sell unapologetically every single day and in multiple places, you'll see your earnings increase significantly.

Remember, each sale you make allows you to positively impact more clients with your life-changing services. By not selling enough, you're essentially withholding your expertise from those who need it most. Even worse, potential clients may turn to your competitors and purchase their offers instead.

So, if your goal is to get paid daily, consider this your tough-love reminder: you must sell every day. If you're not actively promoting your offerings, your ideal clients will seek out alternatives, resulting in missed opportunities and hundreds of thousands left on the table. This isn't your ideal clients' fault; it's yours. **It's time to step up and sell more.**

Confidence and conviction in your expertise and your offer will set you apart from the noise of the very noisy online space. It enables you to showcase your expertise and build trust with your audience whilst positioning yourself as the authority. When people perceive you as the authority in your industry, you become influential in their decision-making, especially when it comes to buying, and it makes it easier and faster for them to buy from you. This speeds up the buyer's journey and the speed at which someone can go from finding you for the first time to buying from you. Now is the perfect opportunity to revisit the four Cs discussed in Chapter Two. Remember, the more confidence you have in yourself as the expert and conviction in your offers, the easier it will be to make sales.

If you're anything like my clients and me, you'll be ready to speed up your sales process so that your potential high-level clients are already sold on working with you before they reach out. This is where your marketing content becomes the deal breaker. Your marketing content will be the difference between sales feeling slow and heavy and sales that are fast, where people find and go on to buy from you quickly, sometimes on the same day. This is why your marketing content, including your social media posts, should be treated like a shop window. Your audience should instantly understand who you are and what you offer as soon as they visit your account.

I teach a three-pillar content funnel designed to position you as an authority in your niche and turn new followers into paying clients:

The first pillar is growth content. Problem-awareness content makes up a significant part of this, where you highlight your ideal clients' current struggles and their desired outcomes while showcasing what they could be doing better or the key element they're missing, highlighting your unique method and offer as the vehicle to help them achieve their goals.

The second pillar is nurture content. Most of this is connection-building content, where storytelling plays a crucial role, allowing your ideal clients to self-identify in you and see themselves reflected in your journey and that of your clients.

Finally, the third pillar is conversion content. This is largely activating content, which empowers your ideal clients to take action and make a purchase.

The more tailored and specific your content is to your ideal, high-ticket client, the more effectively it will resonate with them, leading to quicker conversions. Your content will do the heavy lifting for your sales, building interest and desire in your ideal clients even before they reach out. Your goal is to create content that ensures your ideal, high-ticket clients are already sold on you and your offers before they even enquire. In other words, they're already in and it's time to welcome those daily Stripe notifications!

Whilst showing up and taking up space in your industry as a leader and as the authority is powerful and will significantly impact how your ideal, high-ticket clients interact with and buy from you, you need a solid but simple client pathway and profitable product suite in place that makes buying your next thing easier and the most obvious next step for your ideal, high-ticket clients. This means having the right infrastructure in place where you have a profitable product suite that supports your ideal clients at the different stages of their journeys and financial accessibility, as we covered in Chapter Seven.

THE BIG MISCONCEPTION AROUND HIGH-TICKET BUYERS

There's a common misconception about converting high-paying clients: many entrepreneurs believe that these clients are only interested in jumping straight into the highest-priced offers possible. Contrary to this belief, that's not always the case. Sometimes, high-ticket buyers want to know what it's like to work with you on a smaller offer before they make the big jump. They want to date you for a bit, before jumping straight in and getting married. A powerful strategy I've found to be effective for filling my high-ticket offers is to first give my ideal clients a taste of what it's like to work with me by delivering a micro offer.

Micro offers have several advantages. With a lower price point, they attract a larger volume of clients, making it easier for you to build momentum. These offers are designed to focus deeply on one specific strategy, enabling clients to achieve quick wins. This not only helps to build trust rapidly but also provides you with valuable social proof that you can leverage to generate curiosity and intrigue around your higher-priced offers. By creating this initial connection, you can convert more clients into your premium offerings, ultimately impacting more people at once.

Once the micro offer is running, the aim is to deliver as much value as possible to enable more quick wins for your clients to speed up the buying process by building know, like and trust faster than using other strategies. On the back end of a micro offer, with a simple up-sell funnel in place, you can drive more qualified leads into your other offers, including your higher ticket offers, which fill up fast, because you've already built know, like and trust with the clients by supporting them and giving them value inside your micro offer.

The key takeaway I want to give you to help make sales easier before we dive deeper into understanding high-ticket sales is to simply not overcomplicate sales because business and high-ticket sales get to be simple when you know how.

UNDERSTANDING HIGH-TICKET SALES

For consistent high-ticket sales to become the norm in your business, you need to understand your ideal, high-ticket client inside out and your messaging needs to be magnetic and speak specifically and only to them for them to convert into paying clients. You know this because we've already done lots of this throughout this book. Hint: there's a reason why it keeps coming up — it's important!

High-ticket clients buy differently, making them a different ballgame when it comes to buyer psychology compared to those who invest in low- and mid-ticket offers. They typically don't require persuasion or handholding through the buying process. Often, they've already decided that you are the expert they want to work with before they even reach out to inquire about your services.

This insight means that your marketing, messaging and content should be tailored to speak directly to clients who are ready to move and take action. As you know, these clients are both problem-aware and solution-aware; they recognise the problem they want to solve and are actively seeking a solution. To attract these clients, use empowering language that inspires them to take action because selling to and converting high-ticket clients is significantly easier than dealing with those still stuck in struggle mode and not yet ready to invest.

High-ticket clients buy in their own time which means that often (not always), urgency and scarcity tactics won't work. They are ultimately interested in working in close proximity with you to get a bigger transformation in a faster time frame, in a way that makes getting those results more convenient and where their risk when it comes to the loss of money or time is less by accessing your expertise and support.

It's important when it comes to your marketing to high-ticket clients, that you don't get caught up in vanity metrics such as the number of likes and comments on your content. Most of my high-ticket, multi-five-figure, pay-in-full clients weren't engaging with my content before they started working with me. They often show up out of the blue and tell you that they've been watching you, that they love your work, and they'll ask how they can work with you. So, don't worry about the likes or the lack of them, focus on how you can best serve your audience and clients with the best possible value.

It's essential to understand that high-ticket clients typically aren't always looking for a complete overhaul of their current approach. Instead, they often invest in your services for the micro tweaks and small adjustments you can provide as an expert. These clients are generally already experiencing good results, but they're looking to elevate those outcomes to achieve great results and big transformations. This often comes through the refinement of their existing strategies or practices, enhanced by your support and expertise.

Finally, one of the most important lessons I want you to take away from this book, if you remember nothing else, is the importance of detaching from the outcome of a sale. There's nothing more off-putting and repelling than someone who appears overly keen to sell you something. It screams desperation and scarcity, which definitely doesn't align with a premium brand image. Think back to a time when you were out with friends, enjoying a good time, and someone approached you but wouldn't take the hint to back off. It's clear they have only one thing on their mind: to jump straight to the end without taking the time to connect first. This kind of behaviour is not only off-putting but also screams neediness, which is the polar opposite of the confident, assured persona you want to embody as a high-ticket expert. As we've already covered, maintaining this detachment mindset is essential for your sales success.

Ethical Sales and Influence Techniques

Marketing is all about influencing your audience and encouraging them to buy from you, without the need to actually encourage them. A key component of effective marketing is how you choose to influence your audience. To create a positive and ethical influence, focus on leading with value. This approach shows that you genuinely care about your clients and audience and truly want to help them. It's essential to prioritise long-term goals and lead with authentic connections with potential clients, rather than purely chasing immediate sales. By thinking about and prioritising the elevated impact you can create with your clients and the elevated lifetime value of a client to your business, you set yourself up for sustained success.

BUILDING THE CONFIDENCE FOR HIGH-TICKET SALES

There has been no better or easier time to sell your offers and make money than today, through the power of the internet and specifically, social media. You can create, launch and sell a high-ticket offer in an instant, you can attract new high-ticket clients who you get to impact fast, and new money can land in your bank account almost at the speed of light. The power of social media as a vehicle to grow a business is so vast. It's a free marketing tool which you can use to impact millions and generate the most life-changing sums of money, especially when focusing on high-ticket sales. So, when it comes to those moments where you find yourself feeling stuck on what to say or what to sell on social media and the internet, remind yourself of what a powerful time it is to be alive when it comes to business, creating impact and the potential to make millions. Also, remind yourself that there is no room for doubt when it comes to high-ticket sales.

SELLING THROUGH OBJECTIONS WITH GRACE

People will often have questions and potential objections when considering a new product, offer or service, including high-ticket clients. Addressing these concerns proactively is essential to building trust and credibility with your audience. By anticipating the questions or hesitations they might have, you can infuse these insights into your marketing and sales process. This approach not only reassures potential clients but also demonstrates that you understand their needs and concerns.

Integrating these pre-emptive responses into your content helps to create a smoother buying journey for your ideal, high-ticket clients, allowing your marketing to do the heavy lifting in making the sales process easier. For example, you can create FAQ sections, blog posts, or social media content that directly addresses common objections. This not only positions you as an authority in your field but also empowers your audience to feel more confident and certain in their purchasing decisions. Ultimately, by guiding them through their doubts and questions, you can increase your conversion rates, impact more people, foster long-term relationships with your clients and multiply your sales.

THE PLACES TO SELL YOUR HIGH-TICKET OFFERS

When it comes to selling your offers and services, give yourself permission to let loose and sell everywhere unapologetically. The more your potential high-ticket clients see you sell your offers, the more awareness they have around your offers and services and the more likely they are to buy from you. This can be anywhere from your website, social media platforms, stories, podcasts, virtual and live events and stages. Even the sky is not the limit when it comes to where you can sell your high-ticket offers – you could probably get a banner up there off the back of an aeroplane, they do say that money follows attention!

YOUR NON-NEGOTIABLE DAILY SALES ACTIVITIES

I want to share some non-negotiable daily sales activities that you can implement in your business today to multiply your impact and boost your sales. Before diving into these activities, my first piece of advice is to start your working day by focusing on income-generating tasks. These are the essential activities that directly contribute to your sales and revenue. Whether you handle them yourself as a small business owner or delegate them to your team, make these tasks your top priority each day, as soon as you hit your desk for the day.

Action steps: Here are some key income-generating tasks to incorporate into your daily routine for consistent high-ticket sales:

1. **Set a Sales Target and Track Your Progress:** Establish clear sales goals and monitor how you're doing in relation to them consistently.
2. **Prioritise Daily Selling:** Make selling a non-negotiable part of your daily agenda.
3. **Sell Across Multiple Platforms:** Engage with your potential clients on various platforms every day to maximise your reach.
4. **Follow Up with Unconverted Leads:** Revisit leads that haven't converted yet; timely follow-ups can lead to additional sales.

5. **Implement Daily Lead Generation:** Dedicate time each day to make new connections and generate new leads for your business.

6. **Drive New Conversations:** Actively seek out new conversations each day; this often leads to fresh leads.

7. **Utilise BTS Sales:** Promote additional offerings to clients already within your business ecosystem, as they are much more likely to purchase from you than a colder audience.

8. **Create Additional Offers for Existing Clients:** Offer up-sells, down-sells and cross-sells to maximise revenue from your current client base.

9. **Build Excitement Around Upcoming Offers:** Generate buzz for your new offerings and create waitlists to gauge interest.

10. **Implement Trust Funnels:** Set up trust funnels behind your offers to fill your mid- and high-ticket sales more effectively.

By integrating these activities into your daily routine, you'll create a robust foundation for consistent sales growth and increased client engagement.

My clients learn to sell unapologetically when working with me. They understand that sales are service, and that to get paid often, they need to be selling often. With this mindset shift and change in attitude towards sales, we see their sales skyrocket.

To bring everything together from this chapter, mastering premium sales strategies is essential for creating a thriving business that not only meets your financial goals but also delivers immense value to your clients. By focusing on understanding your ideal client's needs, crafting irresistible offers and engaging in ethical selling practices, you position yourself as a trusted, go-to expert in your field. Remember, selling high-ticket offers is not just about closing a client; it's about building meaningful relationships and providing transformative solutions that elevate your clients' lives. Embrace the practices outlined in this chapter, remain committed to your growth and watch as you multiply your impact and income.

ACCESS YOUR EXCLUSIVE HIGH-TICKET MASTERY MINI-COURSE

Simply go to **bit.ly/Highticketmethodbookcourse** to access your Chapter Ten resources and for more consolidation on premium sales strategies.

ELEVEN
ACTIVATING YOUR HIGH-TICKET FUTURE

Congratulations! You've made it to the final chapter and 'wrap up' of *The High-Ticket Method*®, and that, in itself, is a life-changing milestone. By making it this far you're already 95% closer than most to multiplying your impact and income in your business using the power of high-ticket sales and you're doing it all ethically and with integrity. Throughout this book, you've learned about the foundations of high-ticket sales: what they are, how to ethically craft and sell premium power offers which are irresistible for your ideal high-ticket clients, and how to position yourself as the only go-to expert for the high-calibre clients ready to hire and pay you. Now, as we close out this part of our journey together, it's time to pull everything into action to create the elevated impact and income you want. I haven't written this book to be just another book which you read and never implement. Everything I've given you here is significantly impacting my business and the businesses of my clients by elevating the calibre of clients we attract, our impact and income. **You are no different.**

I want to acknowledge that you may still feel hesitant. You've absorbed the strategies, but a part of you might be thinking, *"Can I really do this? Am I ready to step into this new level?"* Let me reassure you: not only are you ready — you're more than capable. The mindset blocks you're encountering are not unique to you, but rather they are a normal part of levelling up in business and are the exact blocks I experienced, and my clients' experience right before they start implementing these powerful strategies with me. But, like me, they choose to raise the bar and lead, even when it feels uncomfortable, and the results on the other side of this implementation are game-changing. Because you are here, you are no different.

OVERCOMING YOUR FINAL HURDLES

It's very likely that your mindset monkeys and doubts are creeping in again right now, casting doubt over the excitement you initially felt when you first started thinking about getting more of the high-ticket clients you want and earning more than ever in your business. You may wonder if your audience is truly ready to invest in high-ticket offers, or whether you have the authority to charge premium prices. Let me remind you again that these thoughts are completely normal. Mindset challenges are usually the biggest hurdle when it comes to elevating the calibre of client you want to attract and being paid more for the work you love without multiplying your workload. Whether these are mindset challenges focused on fear of failure or simply not knowing if this will work for you, remember that your subconscious will always be there and showing up when you commit to trying something new. It's normal. You are not alone. As we discussed earlier, you don't have consistent high-ticket clients because you haven't positioned yourself to have them yet. Let's not make it more complicated than that. **Remember, business is simple, we don't need to overcomplicate it.**

Here's the truth: your expertise, your existing results, your journey and your ability to co-create life-changing transformations with your clients are enough. Trust me, I've done this work with enough clients to know this. Using the strategies

I've given you in this book, you now know how to attract your ideal, high-ticket clients and how to elevate the perceived value of you, your brand and your offers so that your work becomes irresistible to the right high-ticket clients. Clients who see value in you will invest and those who don't are simply not your target audience. Your focus, moving forward, should be on those who are ready to pay for the game-changing value you bring to the table. High-ticket clients don't just buy services; they buy exclusivity, outcomes, transformation and a deeper level of commitment, and you're the one to guide them.

YOUR ACTION PLAN: HOW TO IMPLEMENT EVERYTHING YOU'VE LEARNED

As you close this book, I want to make sure you're fully equipped to take action because, as you know, that's where real change happens. Here's a straightforward, actionable plan to get you started and to get you results which you can use alongside your exclusive book course which you can access at bit.ly/ Highticketmethodbookcourse.

1. Create a Mindset Reset

Before you can fully embrace high-ticket sales, it's essential to reset your mindset around money and value. Remind yourself that charging premium prices doesn't just benefit you, it benefits your clients. Higher investments usually lead to higher emotional and financial commitment by your clients, which results in better outcomes for them and, as a by-product, for you and your business too. The key to elevating and maintaining your mindset is programming your mind for high-ticket sales and elevating your environment because you are a result of your environment. This includes creating and practising daily affirmations focused on your potential, visualisations of your next level identity and what life looks like for your future self, gratitude and surrounding yourself with the people achieving what it is that you want to achieve – people who are on a similar journey to you and who understand and encourage your growth. This can look like immersing yourself in books, podcasts and events and getting the support you need from the right mentors and coaches.

2. Craft Your Magnetic Message

Your messaging is crucial. I guarantee it's the key difference between offers that flop and offers that pop. Crafting messaging which magnetises your ideal, high-ticket clients requires you to speak directly to the high-ticket clients you want to attract, with laser specificity. Get inside their head. Find out what keeps them up at night. How does this impact them? What are the symptoms of this? Where are they currently at and where do they want to be? And what's stopping them from getting there? Use the words they use verbatim, no 'fluffy' clever-sounding language which you think sounds good because it just won't land with them.

Craft messaging that positions you as the expert, highlighting both the emotional and financial ROI your clients will receive. Focus on speaking to the desires more than the pain points of your ideal, high-ticket clients because remember, desire-led marketing brings your ideal clients closer to making their desired results their reality and this, in turn, activates them to take action and invest in your offer. All of this relies on you doing your ideal client work, which we dived deep into in Chapter Three. This work needs to be done right for everything else that you layer on top in your business to succeed. Don't forget that high-ticket clients are not just looking for a service, they're looking for *the* confident expert, trust, transformation and the expert they believe can guide them to their desired result.

3. Create Your POWER Offer

You already know that adding another zero to your price isn't enough and isn't how to go about high-ticket sales. Review your current offers and ask yourself: Does this solve a specific problem for my high-ticket client? Does this offer reflect the big transformation my ideal client wants in the timeframe they want? Use the POWER offer blueprint and personalised experience strategies I've given you to optimise your offers and refine and justify your premium pricing, to make your high-ticket power offers irresistible for your ideal, high-ticket clients. Build the confidence that your offer far exceeds the value of your competitors', by making sure it has clear, tangible outcomes and is designed to elevate your client's life or business significantly. Be sure that it ticks all four expert values – big results, speed of results, convenience and reduced risk. Communicate that your power offer enhances all four expert values, and you have a high-ticket offer which your ideal high-ticket clients will want.

4. Start Talking About Your Offer

One of the biggest mistakes I see entrepreneurs make is hiding their offers. You need to start talking about your high-ticket offer immediately — the faster you do, the faster it will sell. Don't leave it for months down the line because you think everything will then be 'ready'. Prioritise progress over perfection and start talking about and selling your power offer as soon as you have its foundations nailed (and no, you don't need all modules or resources recorded or created before you sell it!). This doesn't mean being pushy but it does mean being visible and consistent. Mention it across your marketing ecosystem, in your emails, social media and during conversations with potential clients. The more you talk about it, the more comfortable you'll feel and the more clients will see you as the go-to expert that they need.

5. Reach Out to Potential Clients

Use the strategies in this book to start reaching out to your potential high-ticket clients. Whether through networking, referrals or laser-targeted marketing in your content, identify and engage with those who would benefit the most from your offer. Don't wait for clients to come to you, go out and find them.

6. Set Sales Goals and Make Sales

Define clear and measurable sales goals for the next thirty, sixty and ninety days at least. Start with small, attainable goals to build momentum and gradually increase your targets. Keep in mind that your goal is not just to land any client — it's to convert the *right* client. Remember that to achieve your big, audacious money and business goals, you need to be focused on selling the right offers to the right, high-level clients. You're not going to be selling every offer to everyone. We're talking about quality, not quantity. Track your progress with every sale that comes in and celebrate every win, big or small.

7. Extraordinary Results for Your Clients Mean Extraordinary Results for You: Deliver Results Like Never Before

Once you begin landing high-ticket clients, the real work begins. You're committed to converting high-ticket clients and that means delivering a valuable experience and results. Commit to co-creating results with your clients that exceed their expectations. Ask yourself how you can go above and beyond to serve your clients in a way that's both transformational and sustainable. The better results you deliver, the more referrals and higher client retention levels you'll generate by activating the **Clients-and-Cash-on-Repeat system**.

MOVING FORWARD WITH CONFIDENCE

It's important to remember that this book was never just about making money, though that's certainly a big part of the equation and I'm very vocal and frank about that. It's about building a business that serves both you and your clients in a way that's impactful, ethical and wildly scalable. High-ticket sales aren't just about charging more, they're about doing more, transforming lives and creating a ripple effect in your clients, community and industry. High-ticket sales are your ticket to the freedom fueled lifestyle by design that you want.

You now have everything you need to build a premium, high-ticket arm to your business and the strategies you've been given can be applied to any business to multiply its impact and income. The strategies are here, the tools are here and, most importantly, you are here. But none of this will matter unless you take action. The real transformation happens when you step into the role of the in-demand confident expert, own your incredible unique value and start selling your premium power offers with confidence, unapologetically.

BRINGING IT ALL TOGETHER

You've worked hard to get to this point and the journey has only just begun. By mastering high-ticket client attraction and sales, you're not just scaling your business; you're scaling your impact by positively changing the lives of the clients you work with. You're showing up for yourself, your high-ticket clients, your industry and your family in a way that creates real, lasting change. You are not a one-minute, 'flash-in-the-pan' wonder. You are exceptional, sensational and unstoppable and the world needs you and your work.

I want you to finish reading this book with an unstoppable mindset that you can, and you will. To paraphrase Queen, *you won't let anyone stop you now.*

So, I ask you: Are you ready to step into the arena of one, where consistent, high-ticket clients become your reality and you claim the wildly successful impact and income you deserve? Because the next move is yours.

I believe in you. Let's go make it happen.

That concludes ***The High-Ticket Method***®. Now, it's your turn to take everything you've learned and apply it. You've got this. I can't wait to see what you achieve because your success is inevitable.

Tania

REFERENCES

Thoughts, emotions and actions

Ecker, B. (2012). *The Science of the Subconscious Mind: Why You Do What You Do and How to Change It.* University of Cambridge Press.

Mindset: The New Psychology of Success by Carol S. Dweck

Bargh, J. A., & Morsella, E. (2008). "The Unconscious Mind." *Perspectives on Psychological Science, 3(2), 73–79.* DOI:10.1111/j.1745-6916.2008.00063.

Positive Psychology

Gable and Haidt, (2005) *What (and Why) is Positive Psychology? In The Oxford Handbook of Positive Psychology*

SMART goals

Doran, G. T. (1981). *There's a S.M.A.R.T. Way to Write Management's Goals and Objectives. Management Review,70(11),* 35-36

AUTHOR BIO

Dr Tania King-Mohammad is a former NHS Radiologist who, after suffering burnout and borderline depression due to the extreme pressures of the healthcare industry, swapped scrubs and clinics for financial freedom and wealth. She went from thousands of £££ in credit card debt to life and financial freedom through building a £seven-figure property portfolio and as a successful high-ticket sales and business strategist.

As a mother of two young children, who has emigrated from the UK to Ibiza, she brings a unique perspective on balancing professional ambition with family life.

A highly respected, leading high-ticket sales expert, a certified business strategist and a certified positive psychology coach, with clients internationally, Dr Tania is a sought-after, high-ticket sales mentor for ambitious leading entrepreneurs ready to multiply their impact and income by scaling with premium clients, ethically. She now dedicates her time to supporting clients across the globe on how to attract and convert high-ticket clients consistently, thereby elevating their impact and income for an extraordinary business and an ultimate freedom lifestyle built by design.

You can connect with her on:

@freedomwithtania

@freedomwithtania

www.taniakingmohammad.com